FROM SEA & STREAM

LOU SEIBERT PAPPAS

Illustrations By
Marinell & Robert Harriman

101 Productions
San Francisco

Note: Measurements in this book are not straight
conversions from U.S. measurements to metric, but
have been adapted into metric for each individual recipe.

COVER DESIGN: Lynne O'Neil
COVER PHOTOGRAPH: Rik Olson

The first edition of this book was published
with the title *International Fish Cookery*.
This edition has been revised to include the
many varieties of fish new to the market.

Published by 101 Productions, 834 Mission Street,
San Francisco, California 94103.
Distributed to the book trade in the United States by
The Macmillan Publishing Company, New York.

Library of Congress Cataloging-in-Publication Data

Pappas, Lou Seibert.
      From sea and stream.

      Originally published: International fish cookery.
San Francisco : 101 Productions, c1979.
      Includes index.
      1. Cookery (Fish)   2. Cookery (Shellfish)
I. Title.
TX747.P36   1986   641.6'92   86-18171
ISBN 0-89286-266-1

Contents

A World of Fish

The world plays host to a wealth of fish specialties. My remembrances of superb fish feasts, from ultra-simple to complex, span continents and decades:

A childhood favorite, and a challenge to finish: crab Louis on the Oregon coast. A campfire celebration of salmon fillets barbecued Indian style on the beach. Boiled Maine lobster and Indian pudding at Durgin Park in Boston during a college summer. A career girl splurge: sole Marguery at Jack's, the famous old San Francisco restaurant. Digging Pismo clams, then marvelous clam chowder at a Santa Cruz beach cabin. Pompano amandine at Antoine's in New Orleans. The nutty sweetness of macadamia nuts on mahi-mahi in Kona, Hawaii. A San Juan Island shellfish barbecue, unforgettable because of the succulence of the seafood and the beauty of the setting.

A new world of fish cookery discovered in the Old World: *gravlax* with mustard sauce at the elegant Operakällaren restaurant in Stockholm. A croustade of crayfish tails, a brochette of broiled shrimp with béarnaise sauce, and coquilles St. Jacques Thermidor from a Swedish table. Smoked salmon *smørrebrød* with caviar and grated horseradish in Denmark. A brimming platter of scarlet crayfish accompanied with icy aquavit in Helsinki. Fish at the great three-star French restaurants: salmon in champagne at La Pyramide in Vienne, salmon in sorrel sauce at Hotel des Frères Troisgros in Roanne, and salmon under a golden soufflé at Auberge de L'Ill in Alsace. Bouillabaisse with its accompanying giant platter of fish at Madame Garac's in Nice. The glorious array of cold marinated seafood *antipasti* at the Royal Danieli in Venice: mussels, crayfish, octopus, tuna, shrimp, and *granceola,* the sweet-meated Italian crab. Over-sized Greek lobster at a seaside cafe in the pretty resort town of Aghios Nikolaos on Crete. Stuffed mussels bought from a street vendor to begin a poached fish dinner at a fishermen's restaurant in Istanbul.

More recently: superb ceviche at the contemporary El Padellon de Caza Restaurant in Lima, Peru. The squid, octopus, and celery root salad at the waterfront restaurant Zio Ciccio in Marsala, Sicily. Enormous spicy fried prawns at Henri's Galley in Macao and neck of giant clam at Sun Tung Lok, Hong Kong. The magnificent truffled lobster ravioli in champagne sauce at the Waterside Inn, Bray-on-Thames, England. Closer to home, sashimi and sushi star: none is better than yellow-tail tuna paired with an avocado fan bathed in gingered vinaigrette from Wolfgang Puck's Spago in Los Angeles.

And underlying all these memories, the magnificent clean taste of the sea and the stream.

Lou Seibert Pappas
Palo Alto, California

FISH STORIES

For as long as humankind has inhabited the earth, fish has been a prized source of food. Bones of salmon have been unearthed in cave dwellings in southern Europe dating back to 25,000 B.C., and salmon are depicted in Stone Age cave paintings in France. Artifacts from the Columbia River watershed indicate that North American Indians living there around 11,000 B.C. cherished salmon both as a basic food and as a mythological creature.

Fish has played an important part in the mythology, religion, art, and medicine of many human cultures. In ancient Egypt fish were given godly status because of their watery existence, suspended between heaven and earth, and mummified bodies of Nile perch have been found in the tombs of pharaohs. The organs of fish were believed by the ancients to have curative powers: Pliny and Galen advised that the brains of a shark, boiled in oil, would cure a toothache or the bite of a dog. Fish was thought to be useful against viper bites, and creamed pike was used to dress wounds.

Fish is an age-old symbol of fertility, and even today the roe of herring is used in a Buddhist nuptial ceremony to insure many children. Another of the special properties long associated with fish has been its alleged power as an aphrodisiac. Many ancient religious cults forbade their priests to eat fish, while encouraging the rest of the people to consume quantities. Even now, raw oysters are believed by some to be an aphrodisiac.

FISH AS A HEALTH FOOD

Today fish is increasingly prized for its high nutritional value. It is one of the best sources of high-quality protein available to us, because it has a lower calorie content than meat and is generally much lower in saturated fat.

The calorie content of fish varies according to the fat content. Fish varies considerably in fat content and may be divided into three categories: lean, moderately fatty, and fatty fish. A large majority of fish fall into the lean category, having an average of 2 percent fat (a range of .1 to 3.9 percent). Moderately fatty fish contain approximately 6 percent fat (a range of 4 to 8.9 percent). Fatty fish contain approximately 12 percent fat (a range of 9 percent or more). A 4-ounce (125 g) serving of a lean fish such as halibut, mahi-mahi, haddock, hake, sole, or turbot contains approximately 100 calories. A moderately fatty fish such as albacore, sea trout, or swordfish contains approximately 130 calories per 4-ounce serving. A fatty fish such as butterfish, mackerel, coho salmon, shad, or lake trout contains approximately 240 calories per 4-ounce serving. Contrast this with an average count of 320 calories for 4 ounces of lean meat, and it is apparent that even the "fattest" of fish are considerably lower in calories than an equivalent amount of lean meat, while supplying approximately the same amount of protein.

Lean and moderately fatty fish supply somewhat less protein than an equivalent amount of lean meat: 5.5 grams of protein for 1 ounce of fish compared with 7 grams for 1 ounce of meat. Fatty fish are almost equivalent to lean meat, with 6.4 grams of protein per ounce. Shellfish vary more widely in protein level: Oysters have 2.4 grams of protein per ounce, clams 3.1, and crab and lobster 4.9. Shrimp is the shellfish highest in protein with 6.6 grams of protein per ounce.

It is important to note that the protein in fish is of a very high quality, that is, it has a generous number and a wide range of the amino acids that the body needs for growth and for healing. Oysters, for example, though their actual protein content is relatively low, have a quality of protein that is actually higher than that of beef as well as that of most other fish. The protein in fish is also highly digestible—slightly more so than the protein in beef or chicken. And of the fat contained in fish, a high proportion is in the form of high-quality polyunsaturated fatty acids, which are believed to reduce the level of cholesterol in the blood.

Lean and moderately fatty fish and oysters and clams are lower in cholesterol content than meat; 1 ounce of lean meat has 25 grams of cholesterol, while both lean and moderately fatty fish have 19 grams of cholesterol per ounce; oysters have only 13 grams of cholesterol per ounce, clams 14 grams. Fatty fish, however, have 24 grams of cholesterol per ounce, almost the same as lean meat, while crab and lobster have more, with 28 grams, and shrimp has a grand total of 42 grams of cholesterol per ounce. If cholesterol is a problem, then choose fish in preference to meat, but avoid fatty fish, crab, lobster, and shrimp.

Fish are generally low in sodium. Saltwater fish have no higher sodium content than fresh-water fish. If you are concerned with sodium content, avoid all smoked fish and salt cod—these have had salt added as part of the curing process. Among shellfish, oysters and soft-shelled clams are low in sodium; hard-shelled clams and lobster are considerably higher.

Fish is an excellent source of minerals, including iodine, magnesium, calcium, phophorous, iron, potassium, copper, and fluoride. Fish in general is a good source of B complex vitamins. Some fatty fish are high in vitamin D, and swordfish and whitefish are high in vitamin A.

THE FISH MARKET

A decade ago just six species—salmon, tuna, flounder, cod, shrimp, and lobster—accounted for more than 60 percent of the fish consumed in the United States. Today the figures have changed as consumers enjoy a much wider variety of fish. Increased demand for seafood has caused these traditional species to become overfished, while pollution helped diminish the supply. These factors, plus inflation, have caused prices to skyrocket.

Less familiar fish that have long been prized in other countries are coming to market in the United States. These include hake, pollock, whiting, shark, mackerel, mullet, croaker, squid, and grouper. New Zealand and Hawaii are supplying pompano, orange roughy, ahi, wahoo (or ono), mahi-mahi, and opaka-paka. Sea bass is coming from Chile, sole from Holland, and salmon from Norway. Other newly marketed fish include scrod (or cusk), monkfish, sablefish, bluefish, and the lemon sole, gray sole, and dab sole from New England. Shellfish new to the marketplace include the "pink singing" scallops from the Pacific Northwest and the many new premium breeds of half-shell oysters from the West Coast.

FISH COOKERY AROUND THE WORLD

Some of the first recipes set down in writing describe methods of cooking fish. In *The Deipnosophists,* or *Banquet of the Learned,* Athenaeus, an Egyptian Greek of the third century A.D., suggests strewing shark with cumin and "what fragrant herbs the garden gives."

Since those words were written, almost every ethnic group on earth has developed a characteristic way of cooking the kinds of fish available to it. Nomadic cultures and early civilizations grilled fish over open fires or baked fish in coals, and today we have a legacy of grilled or broiled and baked fish recipes from all over the world; many of the best originated in Mediterranean regions, where fish were cooked with pungent native herbs such as fennel, thyme, and bay leaves.

Most countries with an abundance of fish have evolved national fish soups or stews similar to the Mediterranean bouillabaisse. Some nationalities have developed a particularly light touch in sautéeing their native fish, such as the French and the Italians, and the even swifter Oriental method of stir-frying is a variation of this technique.

The method of cooking foods by steam without immersion in liquid was also developed in the Orient—a delicate method of cooking fish that allows all the pure flavor of the fish to come through.

Many of the great French fish dishes are based on the technique of poaching, in which fish is covered with liquid and cooked on top of the stove, or half covered with liquid, then covered with paper or foil and cooked in the oven (the latter method is sometimes referred to as braising).

Different methods of preserving fish have resulted in some of the world's most wonderful foods, such as smoked salmon, trout, and eel; pickled herring; anchovies; and salt cod, many of them eaten as appetizers as well as ingredients in main-course dishes. Several countries "cook" or "pickle" raw fish by marinating it several hours in an acid-containing liquid such as lemon or lime juice.

And, of course, some of the most exquisite of all fish dishes consist of fish or fish eggs eaten raw, such as oysters on the half shell, the *sashimi* of Japan, or fresh beluga caviar.

COOKING FISH AT HOME

The trend in cookery today is toward lighter foods, cooked in a more "natural" fashion, without heavy sauces and animal fats, accented by fresh fruits, vegetables, and herbs. The growing popularity of fish is in large part due to its healthfulness, and it plays an important part in the new "cuisines" now popularized by leading French chefs. The speed with which fish cooks is one of its greatest virtues, making it adaptable to simple cooking methods that emphasize the natural taste of the fish, and a perfect choice for the "after 5" cook.

The recipes in this book begin with appetizers and first courses, soups and stews, salads, sauces, luncheon and supper dishes, then main courses organized by cooking techniques: sautéeing and stir-frying; broiling and grilling; poaching and steaming; and baking. There is a brief discussion of each cooking technique at the beginning of its respective section. For a discussion of the basic guidelines for cooking fish, see the end of this section.

In general, it is the fat content of a fish that determines much of its color, flavor and texture and dictates the best cooking method to be used for a particular fish. Lean fish (from .1 to 3.9 percent fat) have much of their richness concentrated in the oils in the liver, and the flesh of the fish is therefore mild in flavor, with a flakier, more tender and whiter flesh than fattier fish ("white-fleshed" is a term that applies to the color of the flesh *after* cooking). Lean fish include sole, halibut, haddock, croaker, lingcod, perch, rockfish, sea bass, smelt, red snapper, whiting, and turbot. These fish are enhanced by cooking methods in which moisture is retained or added, such as poaching, sautéeing, baking in sauces, or simmering in soups.

Fish with a moderate and high fat content (4 to 12 percent or more) have their oil distributed throughout the flesh of the fish, lending the fish a more pronounced flavor; a meatlike, firm texture; and a deeper color than lean fish. These include salmon, swordfish, mackerel, albacore, eel, herring, bluefish, mullet, sablefish, and shad. These fish will stay moist when cooked by quick searing, using relatively high heat, such as broiling and baking without added liquid. They may also be cooked by moist methods as is, for example, salmon, which is so frequently poached.

The cardinal rule of fine fish cookery is *do not overcook.* No amount of cooking will make fish more tender than when it comes from the water: Fish is naturally tender and is cooked only to coagulate the protein and bring out the flavor. The tender and delicate fibers that compose fish and shellfish cook quickly, and overcooking will rob them of their succulent juices and produce a dry and flabby texture.

Upon heating, the flesh of a fish will turn from translucent to opaque. Fish is cooked when the flesh is opaque throughout and the flesh separates gently when pierced with a fork; the fish should retain most of its juices. A good basic rule for all fish cookery is to allow 10 minutes of cooking time for fish that is 1 inch (3 cm) thick at its thickest part when the fish is lying flat; this formula is reliable for any cooking technique. See page 13 for information on cooking frozen fish.

Handling the Catch

BUYING AND STORING FRESH FISH

When buying fresh fish at the market, look for these characteristics indicating freshness: shiny, bright, clear eyes; firm and elastic flesh; bright red gills rather than muddy gray ones; almost no discernible odor, and certainly not a "fishy" one; and a bright, unblemished skin color.

Fish should be refrigerated at 35° to 40°F (3° to 5°C) in a leakproof wrapper as soon as possible after purchase. It should be cooked within two days.

STORING, THAWING, AND COOKING FROZEN FISH

When buying frozen fish, select undamaged packages that feel solid. Store in the the freezer in the original vapor- and moisture-proof wrapper. Keep solidly frozen until ready to thaw. Plan to use frozen fish within 3 months; shellfish and fatty fish are best if kept frozen not longer than 2 months.

Frozen fish should be thawed slowly, and never thawed at room temperature. Thaw in the refrigerator, still in its wrapping, allowing 24 hours for a 1-pound (500 g) package. Thawing time may be shortened by immersing fish (still wrapped) in a bowl of cold water, outside the refrigerator. Use fish as soon as possible after thawing; never hold thawed fish longer than 24 hours.

Frozen fish may be cooked by moist-cooking methods without being thawed; allow double the amount of cooking time specified for unfrozen fish.

CLEANING FISH

Commercially caught and marketed fish are handled quickly and expertly to provide the highest quality and freshest tasting product; fish caught by sportsmen demand the same kind of care. Cleaning a fish at the site is essential, as the digestive enzymes in most fish are extremely powerful. Unless the fish is gutted ("drawn") immediately these enzymes will continue to work, creating spoilage.

First kill the fish by hitting it on the head with a blunt instrument, or break the backbone by hitting it on the edge of a boat or other hard, sharp object. Use a sharp knife to slit the stomach open without breaking into the entrails, which are contained in a pouch. Cut the opening toward the head, then toward the tail, and remove the entrails and discard. If the fish is a female in the right season, there may be roe: minute eggs encased in a membrane. Male fish may contain creamy milt, or sperm, sometimes called "white roe." Though the roe of some fish, such as the gar and the trunkfish, is toxic, most roes are edible. Remove the roe carefully in one piece, wash off, and ice.

If possible, have an ice chest to store fish. If not, use a wicker creel, as it will allow free circulation of air;

separate fish in the creel with grass or ferns. Do not store fish in a creel for longer than 3 hours. For the homeward journey, remove fish from the creel and wrap them loosely in burlap, leaves, seaweed, newspaper or other moisture-holding material (this will cool the fish quickly) and place in an open ice chest with cracked ice.

The final cleaning, or dressing, of the fish (scaling and finning or other trimming) is best accomplished at home. Lay the fish on several layers of newspaper on top of a cutting board. Holding the fish by its tail, remove the scales by scraping a fish scaler or the edge of a knife along the skin from tail to head; turn the fish over and repeat on the other side. (Note: It is not necessary to scale fish that are to be filleted.) Wash the fish well under cold running water, and dry inside and out with paper towels.

FILLETING OVAL-SHAPED FISH

To fillet an oval-shaped fish (thick through the mid-section, like a trout), cut off the head just back of the gills with a medium-sized, slightly flexible sharp knife. Insert the knife into the fish just behind the head so that the blade rests flat on top of the backbone, and cut the fish in two lengthwise by sliding the knife along the backbone to the tail of the fish. When cut, one half of the fish will contain the backbone. Remove the backbone by sliding the knife just under the bone from the head end to the tail.

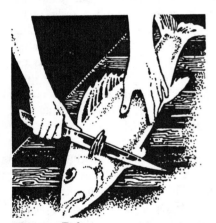

Cleaning Fish

Filleting Oval-Shaped Fish

Filleting Flat Fish

Cut off fins and any bony edges. With skin side down, slide the knife just under the flesh of the fish to remove the fillets from the skin.

FILLETING FLAT FISH

With a medium-sized, slightly flexible sharp knife, make a slanting vertical cut through the flesh just behind the head of the fish, stopping when the knife reaches the backbone. Turning the knife so that it rests flat on top of the backbone, release the top fillet by sliding the knife from the head end to the tail, then cut through the skin at the top of the fish. Turn the fish over and repeat for the second fillet. With skin side down, cut the flesh from the skin of each fillet by sliding the knife just under the flesh. You may divide each fillet in half along the natural line dividing each fillet lengthwise, or leave the fillets whole.

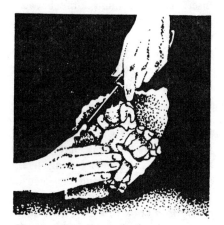

Cleaning Dungeness Crab

You may find it easier to skin very flat fish, such as sole, before filleting: Make a cut across the end of the tail to release the skin from the flesh and, holding the end of the tail in one hand and the tip of the skin in the other, pull the skin off and discard; repeat on the other side. If the fish is to be filleted, cut the flesh along both sides of the natural line dividing the fillet lengthwise, then release the two sections from the backbone by sliding a thin flexible knife underneath them; repeat on the other side.

BUTTERFLY-FILLETING FISH

Cut off head and tail of fish. Cut open the belly of the fish its full length. Slide the blade of a medium-sized, slightly flexible sharp knife between the flesh and the backbone on both sides of the bone to release the flesh, then cut the bone away from the flesh at the top of the fish without breaking through the flesh and skin. Cut the backbone out of the fish at both ends of the fish and lift it out. Press the two halves of the fish apart so that it lies flat.

PREPARING FISH FOR STUFFING

Leave head and tail on the fish. Enlarge the opening on the belly at each end but leave head and tail intact. Slide the blade of a medium-sized, slightly flexible sharp knife between the flesh and the backbone on both sides of the bone to release the flesh, then cut the bone away from the flesh at the top of the fish without breaking through the flesh and skin. Cut the backbone out of the fish at both ends of the fish and lift it out.

NOTE: Save fish heads, bones, fins, and other scraps to freeze and save for making fish stock.

CLEANING AND CRACKING DUNGENESS CRABS

Dungeness crabs may be cleaned and cracked before or after cooking. If the crab is to be cleaned before cooking, you may kill the crab almost instantly by placing it upside down on a cutting board, then holding a sharp heavy knife or cleaver so that the blade rests sharp side down in the center of the crab's underside. Hit the knife or cleaver a sharp blow with a hammer. Wash the crab well under cold running water. To clean and crack, twist claws and legs off, then pry and pull off the top shell. Remove and discard the gray gills and the spongy parts. Save the creamy crab "butter" (fat) for a spread, if you like. Crack the body section and the claws and legs with a hammer.

CLEANING SOFT-SHELL BLUE CRABS

Soft-shell crabs may be cleaned and then cooked live; most of the shell is edible. If you prefer, kill the crabs before cleaning by immersing them upside down in a pan of almost boiling water. Wash crabs well under cold running water and place on a cutting board. With a small knife, cut out eyes and head section. Pull up the shell on each side of the crab and cut out the sandbags and gills. Turn the crab upside down and pry up and pull off the pointed central section; the intestinal vein will come out of the crab along with this section.

CLEANING AND CRACKING HARD-SHELL BLUE CRABS

Hard-shell blue crabs may be cleaned before or after cooking. If you are cleaning them before cooking, kill the crabs first by immersing them upside down in almost boiling water, then rinse under cold running water. Clean and crack crabs by twisting off the claws and legs, then place each crab on its back and pry and pull off the pointed center section of the crab's underside; the intestinal vein should come out along with this section. Wedge your thumb or a small knife between the top and bottom shells and pull off the whole top shell. Reserve the roe (found in females and coral in color after cooking) and the light green liver to add to a sauce if you like. Cut out the spongy gills and the sandbags on the sides. Crack the claws with a hammer or mallet and break the legs in half.

CLEANING AND CRACKING LOBSTER

Lobster may be cleaned before or after cooking. If you prefer to kill a live lobster just before cleaning or cooking it, pierce it with a large sharp knife in the underside, close to the chest; this will kill the lobster almost instantly. Wash the lobster well under cold running water. Place the lobster on its back on a cutting board and use a large heavy knife to split it through the middle without breaking through the back shell. Remove the small sand sac (the stomach) just behind the head and pull out the intestinal vein running down to the tail. Save the roe (found in females and coral in color after cooking) and the light green liver, or tomalley, if you like. Crack the claws of the Northern lobster with a hammer. If using a spiny lobster, twist off and discard legs; to remove all meat from the spiny lobster at once, grasp tail and body and bend shell backwards to break it, then pull the meat out of the tail. To cut cooked lobster completely in half for serving, place the lobster on a cutting board, back shell up, and cut through the back shell with a large, heavy knife.

PREPARING LOBSTER TAILS FOR COOKING

For a "piggyback" lobster tail, cut the upper shell down the center with heavy kitchen scissors, leaving the tail fan intact, and lift the meat up through the slit to rest on the shell. For a butterflied lobster tail, cut through the upper shell, leaving the undershell intact, and press the halves apart so that the tail lies flat. For a "fancut" lobster tail, cut through the clear ribbed undershell on both sides with a small pair of scissors, leaving the tail fan intact; discard the undershell.

SOAKING CLAMS AND MUSSELS

To remove any sand inside clams and mussels, soak them in clear sea water or a mixture of 1-1/2 tablespoons (25 ml) salt and 4 cups (1 L) tap water for 30 minutes, changing the water after the first 10 minutes of soaking, and again after 20 minutes. Scrape off any barnacles from the mussels and cut off beards with a sharp knife (mussels are often sold already de-bearded). Discard any clams or mussels that are broken. Some clams or mussels may be slightly opened; discard any that do not close when the inside is poked with a knife.

OPENING RAW CLAMS AND MUSSELS

Insert a strong, blunt knife between the shell halves near the thick end and run the knife between the halves until the muscles holding them together are cut. Pull the shells apart and cut the muscles from the shell to remove the meat.

SKINNING AND CLEANING EEL

Kill the eel by hitting it sharply on the head with a hammer. Using heavy twine, tie a loop around the head of the eel and then anchor the loop securely to a hook or a door knob. With a single-edged razor, cut through the skin around the circumference of the eel just below the neck. Using a pair of pliers, pull the skin from the eel. Slit open the belly of the eel with the razor and remove and discard the intestines.

OPENING RAW OYSTERS

Scrub oysters well under cold running water with a stiff-bristled brush. Hold an oyster, bottom shell down (the more deeply rounded shell is the bottom shell) and the pointed hinge end facing your palm, in a heavy potholder in your left hand. Insert a pointed oyster knife an inch or so away from the hinge end, where the top and bottom shells meet (the bottom shell protrudes slightly from beneath the top shell) and twist the knife until the shells are pried open. Or you may find it easier to insert the knife just at the point of the hinge. When the shell is opened, cut the muscles holding the two shells together, as well as the muscle holding the oyster to the shell. If you are not serving the oysters on the half shell (using the bottom shell), drain them and strain the liquor through cheesecloth to remove any sand.

BUTTERFLYING RAW SHRIMP

Use a small sharp knife to cut through the back of the shrimp from head to tail, without cutting through the inner curve of the shrimp. Gently pull off the shell, leaving the tail attached to the shrimp. Pull or rinse out the intestinal tract, or vein.

DEVEINING SHRIMP

Make a shallow slash along the back of the shrimp. This will reveal the dark line of the intestinal tract, or vein. Remove with the point of the knife.

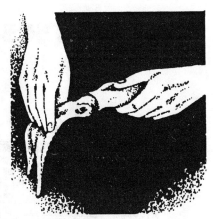
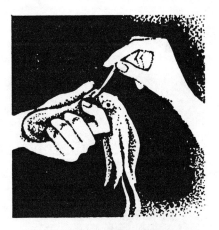

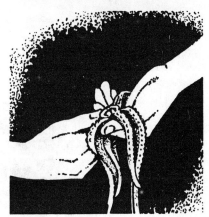

Cleaning Squid

CLEANING SQUID

Wash squid well under cold running water. Holding the pointed tail section in one hand and the base of the tentacles (just below the eyes) in the other, pull gently to separate. Pull out and discard the transparent sword-shaped bone. Remove the ink sac from the innards and save in water if you plan to add it to a sauce. Cut off the tentacles just above the eye section. Discard the eye section and the innards of the body, and rinse out the body. Pop out and discard the small round cartilege at the base of the tentacles. Peel off and discard the transparent speckled membrane, or mantle, covering the tail and body.

Appetizers & First Courses

TARAMOSALATA

In the Greek cuisine, carp roe *(tarama)* is used to flavor mayonnaise made with olive oil. It is often served piled on a plate and adorned with Mediterranean olives to spread on bread or crackers. A more sophisticated presentation calls for dolloping the coral sauce in mushroom caps, or on halved cherry tomatoes or cucumber slices.

2 slices sweet French bread, crusts
    removed
1 jar (4 ounces or 116 g) carp roe or
    red caviar
1/3 cup (75 ml) lemon juice
1 green onion, chopped
1/2 cup (125 ml) each olive oil and
    safflower oil, or 1 cup (250 ml)
    olive oil
Salt and freshly ground black pepper
    to taste
Minced parsley or fresh coriander
Mediterranean olives (optional)
Lavosh (cracker bread), broken into
    pieces, or pita bread, cut into
    wedges, or mushroom caps, halved
    cherry tomatoes, and cucumber
    slices

Place the bread, carp roe, lemon juice, and onion in a blender or a food processor fitted with a steel blade and blend a few seconds. With motor running, gradually pour in oil, blending until thick and creamy. Add salt and pepper and blend again. Empty into a bowl and chill. Sprinkle with parsley just before serving. Serve with olives and lavosh or pita bread or fresh vegetables.
Makes about 2 cups (500 ml)

SMOKED TROUT PÂTÉ

Many fishermen smoke their catch—either commercially or at home. Here is a pâté that utilizes this bounty.

1 pound (500 g) smoked trout,
    skinned, boned, and flaked
3 ounces (75 g) cream cheese, at
    room temperature
1/4 cup (50 ml) half-and-half
1 tablespoon (15 ml) horseradish sauce
1 tablespoon (15 ml) fresh lemon juice
Freshly ground black pepper to taste
2 teaspoons (10 ml) chopped parsley
Danish flatbread or rye crackers
Cucumber slices

Place in a blender or a food processor fitted with a steel blade the trout, cheese, half-and-half, horseradish sauce, lemon juice, pepper, and parsley. Blend until smooth. Spoon into individual serving crocks or ramekins, smoothing the top, and cover and chill until serving time. To serve, spread on flatbread or rye crackers, and cucumber slices.
Makes 6 to 8 appetizer servings

COLD MARINATED TROUT

When the catch is bounteous let wine vinegar and pickling spices give trout pizzazz.

6 small trout
1 tablespoon (15 ml) butter
1 tablespoon (15 ml) safflower oil
1 small onion, thinly sliced
1 cup (250 ml) tarragon-flavored
    white wine vinegar
1 cup (250 ml) water
2 tablespoons (30 ml) dry sherry
2 tablespoons (30 ml) dry white
    wine or vermouth
2 tablespoons (30 ml) mixed pickling
    spices, tied in a small square of
    cheesecloth
Butter lettuce leaves or other salad
    greens

Sauté trout in butter and oil, 1 minute on each side. Place trout and sliced onion in a shallow ceramic or glass dish. In a saucepan heat together the vinegar, water, sherry, wine, and pickling spices. Simmer for 5 minutes. Pour hot marinade over the fish and onion. Let cool, cover, and chill for 2 days, basting occasionally. Remove head, tail, skin, and bones of trout. Serve on a bed of lettuce with the pickled onion slices as a garnish.
Makes 6 first-course servings

GRAVLAX

While touring the stunning blue-tiled kitchen of the Operakällaren restaurant in Stockholm, I witnessed the preparation of *gravlax*. In Scandinavian style, salmon fillets are "cooked" without heat by a marinade of salt and sugar. The marinade penetrates the fish, pulling out moisture and transforming the salmon to a product that closely resembles lightly smoked salmon or kosher-style lox in color and sheen. The rich-tasting slices are nicely balanced by a sprightly mustard-dill sauce. For a party, serve *gravlax* with buttered thinly sliced egg bread and sliced cucumbers, letting guests assemble their own open-face sandwiches.

One 2-1/2 pound (1.25 kg) salmon
    fillet with skin removed from
    one side
2 tablespoons (30 ml) salt
1/4 cup (50 ml) sugar
2 tablespoons (30 ml) brandy or
    cognac
12 black peppercorns
1 tablespoon (15 ml) minced fresh
    dill weed, or
    1 teaspoon (5 ml) crushed dried
    dill weed
Buttered sliced egg bread
Mustard-Dill Sauce, following

Place salmon fillet in a shallow ceramic or glass baking dish. Mix together salt, sugar, brandy, peppercorns, and dill and spoon over the fish. Cover tightly and chill 2 days, basting several times with the accumulating juices. To serve, drain off juices and place fish on a cutting board. Slice very thinly on the diagonal. Overlap salmon slices on buttered bread and spoon Mustard-Dill Sauce over.
Makes about 16 first-course servings

MUSTARD-DILL SAUCE Beat 1 egg yolk in a small bowl with a wire whisk and beat in 2 tablespoons (30 ml) Dijon-style mustard, 4 teaspoons (20 ml) sugar, 1-1/2 tablespoons (25 ml) white wine vinegar, 2 teaspoons (10 ml) fresh lemon juice, 1/2 teaspoon (2 ml) salt, 1-1/2 teaspoons (7 ml) minced fresh dill weed or 1/2 teaspoon (2 ml) crushed dried dill weed, and a dash of white pepper. Gradually beat in 1/4 cup (50 ml) safflower oil. Cover and chill thoroughly. Makes about 3/4 cup (175 ml).

PARISIAN MARINATED SALMON

This exquisite first course or picnic fare is a specialty of Au Petit Montmorency, a one-star Parisian restaurant—they tuck in a few brandied cherries for garnish. Once assembled it will keep under refrigeration for at least a week

2 pounds (1 kg) salmon fillets
1 tablespoon (15 ml) salt
1-1/2 tablespoons (25 ml) sugar
1/2 teaspoon (2 ml) freshly ground
    black pepper
2 onions, thinly sliced
2 lemons, thinly sliced
1/3 cup (75 ml) each fresh lemon juice,
    dry white wine or vermouth, and
    white wine vinegar

Remove any skin from fish and slice across the grain into very thin slices. In a bowl mix together salt, sugar, and pepper. Make a bed of half of the onion and lemon slices in a ceramic or glass baking dish or terrine. Dip salmon slices in the salt mixture and place on top of the vegetables in a single layer. Cover with a layer of the remaining onions and lemons and another layer of salt-coated salmon. Mix together the lemon juice, wine, and vinegar and pour over. Cover and chill 2 days, spooning the juices over the fish several times.
Makes 8 to 10 first-course servings

SASHIMI

Japanese cooks present this appetizer as a striking still life. Use only the very freshest of saltwater fish for *sashimi*—ideally the fish should be caught the same day this dish is served.

1 medium daikon* (about 8 ounces or 250 g)
2-inch (5 cm) piece carrot
1 green onion
12 ounces (375 g) boneless ahi, halibut, sea bass, or albacore
Grated horseradish or ginger root
Parsley sprigs
Soy sauce

Shred daikon into long, fine strands. Shred carrot and mix in. Cut onion lengthwise into slender ribbons 1 inch (3 cm) in length and add. Immerse vegetables in ice water. Cut fish into 1/8-inch-thick (3 mm) slices. Drain vegetables and arrange on a chilled serving platter. Arrange fish on top. Spoon horseradish at one side and place parsley at the other. Serve with a bowl of soy sauce, letting guests blend horseradish with soy sauce to use as a dipping sauce for fish and vegetables.
Makes 4 to 6 appetizer servings

*Large white Japanese radish, available in Japanese markets and some supermarkets.

ABALONE SEVICHE

Another piquant appetizer relies on abalone. It is an ideal prelude to a Mexican party dinner.

1 pound (500 g) abalone steaks
6 tablespoons (90 ml) fresh lime juice
2 tablespoons (30 ml) safflower oil
1/4 cup (50 ml) green chili sauce
1/2 teaspoon (2 ml) salt
1/4 teaspoon (1 ml) freshly ground black pepper
1 garlic clove, minced
1/2 teaspoon (2 ml) sugar
3 drops Tabasco sauce
1 lime, thinly sliced
Fresh coriander sprigs

Pound abalone lightly, then slice into thin strips about 1 inch (3 cm) wide and 1-1/2 inches (4 cm) long. Place in a small ceramic or glass bowl. Mix together the lime juice, oil, chili sauce, salt, pepper, garlic, sugar, and Tabasco sauce. Pour this mixture over abalone and mix well. Cover and chill about 4 hours or overnight. At serving time, spoon into an abalone shell or scallop shells and garnish with lime and coriander sprigs. Pass food picks for serving.
Makes about 16 appetizer servings

MUSSELS WITH GARLIC BUTTER

Each bright orange mussel is tipped with green parsley butter in a pretty first course from Roubatcheff, the two-star restaurant in Chambery, France.

24 mussels
1 shallot or green onion (white part only), chopped
3 garlic cloves, minced
1 tablespoon (15 ml) butter
1/2 cup (125 ml) dry white wine or vermouth
1/4 pound (125 g) unsalted butter, at room temperature
1/4 cup (50 ml) chopped parsley
Dash white pepper

Soak mussels 30 minutes in salted water (see page 16). Scrub mussels well under cold running water with a stiff-bristled brush; cut off beards. In a large soup kettle sauté the shallot and 1 teaspoon (5 ml) of the garlic in the tablespoon (15 ml) of butter until soft. Add wine and mussels. Cover and simmer gently until mussel shells open, about 10 minutes. Discard any mussels that do not open. Remove mussels with a slotted spoon and discard top shells but leave mussels in bottom shells. Arrange in shallow soup bowls and ladle broth over. Beat together unsalted butter, parsley, pepper, and remaining garlic and spread a spoonful at the tip of each mussel.
Makes 4 first-course servings

SPINACH AND CLAMS HIELY

A two-star restaurant in Avignon features this delightful seafood and vegetable dish as a first course. It arrives at tableside in a charming brass-handled copper baking dish.

2 large bunches spinach (about 2
    pounds or 1 kg)
4 tablespoons (60 ml) butter
3 shallots or green onions (white part
    only), chopped
1/4 cup (50 ml) flour
2 cans (7 ounces or 196 g each)
    minced clams with juice
1/2 cup (125 ml) dry white wine or
    dry vermouth
1/2 cup (125 ml) heavy cream
3/4 teaspoon (4 ml) salt
1-1/2 teaspoons (7 ml) chopped fresh
    tarragon, or
    1/2 teaspoon (2 ml) crushed dried
    tarragon
2 ounces (50 g) Gruyère or Jarlsberg
    cheese, shredded (about 1/2 cup
    or 125 ml)
1 ounce (25 ml) Parmesan or
    Romano cheese, grated (about
    1/4 cup or 50 ml)

Wash spinach well under cold running water; do not dry. Place in a large frying pan, cover, and cook until limp. Squeeze out excess moisture and mince. In a saucepan, melt butter and sauté shallots until limp. Add flour and cook 2 minutes, stirring. Drain liquid from clams and stir in. Add wine and cream, and cook and stir until thickened. Season with salt and tarragon and mix in spinach, clams, and Gruyère cheese. Spoon into 6 small ramekins or scallop shells. Sprinkle with Parmesan cheese. Bake in a preheated 400°F (210°C) oven for 15 minutes or until the cheese melts.
Makes 6 first-course servings

HAKKA SNOW CRAB CLAWS

This exotic appetizer is from the Hakka Chinese cuisine. Traditionally one of ten dishes in an elaborate banquet, consider serving it in a simpler context as well, perhaps as a midsummer entrée with a mushroom and watercress salad, chilled whole artichokes, and a gingered melon compote.

1 pound (500 g) medium shrimp,
    shelled and deveined
2 tablespoons (30 ml) sea salt
1/2 cup (125 ml) minced canned
    water chestnuts
1/2 teaspoon (2 ml) salt
Dash white pepper
8 snow crab claws (about 1 pound or
    500 g)
8 cups (2 L) peanut or corn oil
2 egg whites
2 tablespoons (30 ml) cornstarch
Parsley sprigs
Lemon and lime slices

Place shrimp in a bowl, add salt and rub and squeeze the salt into the shrimp with your fingers. Place shrimp in a colander and let cold water run through them for 10 minutes to firm the texture. Pat completely dry with paper towels. Using the dull side of a cleaver pound the shrimp to a paste. Mix in water chestnuts, salt, and pepper.

Each snow crab claw should have half of its shell attached. Knock off the attached half-shell, using a cleaver, but leave the top of the claw on for a "handle." Divide shrimp paste into 8 portions. Take 1 portion and pat into a thin layer, on a sheet of waxed paper, then wrap the crab claws in the shrimp paste. Repeat until all the crab claws are wrapped. Heat oil in a heavy pot or a deep-fat fryer to 400°F (210°C). Meanwhile, mix egg whites with cornstarch, mixing until smooth. Dip crab claws in the egg white mixture and deep-fry them until golden brown. Place on a heated platter and garnish with parsley and sliced lemon and lime.
*Makes 8 appetizer servings or
4 entrée servings*

COQUILLES ST. JACQUES

An elegant first course for a festive meal.

1 cup (250 ml) dry white wine or
    vermouth
1/2 teaspoon (2 ml) crushed dried
    thyme, 1 parsley sprig, and 1 bay
    leaf, tied in a small square of
    cheesecloth
1 pound (500 g) scallops
Salt and white pepper
2 shallots or green onions (white part
    only), chopped
6 ounces (175 g) mushrooms, sliced
3 tablespoons (45 ml) butter
1 teaspoon (5 ml) fresh lemon juice
2 tablespoons (30 ml) flour
1 egg yolk mixed with
3 tablespoons (45 ml) heavy cream
Bread crumbs
1 ounce (25 g) Parmesan cheese,
    grated (about 1/4 cup or 50 ml)

Bring wine to a boil with herbs and add scallops, salt, and pepper; simmer for 6 to 8 minutes, or until scallops turn opaque. Drain, reserving broth, and cut scallops into small pieces. In a large frying pan sauté shallots and mushrooms in 1 tablespoon (15 ml) of the butter and the lemon juice just until glazed, about 1 minute. Melt remaining butter in a saucepan and blend in flour; cook and stir 2 minutes, not allowing flour to brown. Pour in reserved scallop broth and any juices from the mushrooms and cook until thickened, stirring occasionally. Add egg-cream mixture and cook a few minutes longer. Stir in scallops and mushrooms and spoon into 4 buttered scallop shells. Sprinkle with crumbs and cheese. Bake in a preheated 425°F (220°C) oven just until lightly browned, about 10 minutes.
Makes 4 first-course servings

SCALLOP SEVICHE

Seviche is a superb first course for a Latin-American party dinner. Or present it in avocado halves as the main course for a summer supper.

1-1/2 pounds (750 g) scallops
1/2 cup (125 ml) fresh lemon juice
1/2 cup (125 ml) fresh lime juice
2 canned peeled green chilies, seeded
    and chopped
Dash green chili sauce or Tabasco
    sauce
1/4 cup (50 ml) thinly sliced green
    onions
2 large tomatoes, peeled, seeded, and
    chopped
1 teaspoon (5 ml) salt
1 teaspoon (5 ml) chopped fresh
    oregano, or
      1/4 teaspoon (1 ml) crushed dried
      oregano
1/4 cup (50 ml) olive oil
Chopped pimiento and fresh coriander

If using sea scallops, cut them in quarters. Place scallops in a ceramic or glass bowl. Pour lemon and lime juices over and refrigerate overnight, stirring once or twice. Drain. Add the chopped chilies, chili sauce, green onions, tomatoes, salt, oregano, and oil and mix lightly. To serve, spoon into scallop shells and garnish with pimiento and fresh coriander.
Makes 8 to 10 first-course servings or 6 entrée servings

VARIATION Sole, whiting, turbot, or other mild-flavored fish fillets may be substituted for scallops.

OYSTERS ROCKEFELLER

Antoine's, the celebrated New Orleans restaurant, originated this rich first course around 1899 and named it after the richest man of the era.

Rock salt
16 oysters on the half shell
1 large bunch spinach (about 1 pound or 500 g)
1/4 cup (50 ml) minced celery
1 green onion, minced
2 tablespoons (30 ml) minced parsley
4 tablespoons (60 ml) butter
1 tablespoon (15 ml) anisette or Pernod
Salt and white pepper to taste
1/4 cup (50 ml) fine soft bread crumbs mixed with
1 tablespoon (15 ml) melted butter

Fill 4 pie pans with rock salt and nestle 4 oysters in the shell in each. Wash spinach well and trim stems. Drop spinach into boiling salted water and cook for 30 seconds. Drain, squeeze out excess moisture, and chop. Cook celery, onion, and parsley in butter 5 minutes. Turn mixture into the container of a blender or a food processor fitted with a steel blade. Add spinach and anisette and purée. Season with salt and pepper. Spoon spinach over each oyster, spreading to cover, and sprinkle with buttered crumbs. Bake in a preheated 450°F (230°C) oven for 6 to 8 minutes, or until heated through and crumbs are browned.
Makes 4 first-course servings

CRYSTAL PRAWNS

These crystal-clear glazed shrimp are from the Hakka Chinese restaurant kitchen of Mimie Tse, in Mountain View, California. The use of sea salt rather than soy sauce in this cuisine emphasizes the fresh flavor of the sea.

1 pound (500 g) jumbo shrimp, shelled and deveined
2 tablespoons (30 ml) sea salt
8 cups (2 L) peanut or corn oil
1 teaspoon (5 ml) cornstarch
1/2 teaspoon (2 ml) salt
Dash white pepper
1/4 cup (50 ml) water
1/4 cup (50 ml) finely shredded carrots
1/4 cup (50 ml) finely shredded green onions

Place shrimp in a bowl, add salt, and rub and squeeze the salt into the shrimp with your fingers. Place shrimp in a colander and let cold running water run through them for 10 minutes to firm the texture. Bring a large kettle of water to a boil, add shrimp, and cook 45 seconds; drain and dry with paper towels. Heat oil in a heavy kettle or deep-fat fryer to 400°F (210°C). Add shrimp and cook 30 seconds; remove and drain. Mix together in a small bowl the cornstarch, salt, pepper, and water. Heat a wok or frying pan until very hot, add shrimp and quickly stir in cornstarch mixture, cooking until shrimp are coated with a crystal-clear glaze. Turn out on a plate strewn with carrots and onions.
Makes 8 to 10 appetizer servings

SHRIMP AND ROMANO TRIANGLES

Spread Italian-style shrimp paste on toasted bread for last-minute hot canapes. It can be made in seconds with a food processor and kept refrigerated until ready to use.

4 ounces (125 g) cooked small shrimp
4 ounces (125 g) Romano cheese, grated (about 1 cup or 250 ml)
4 tablespoons (60 ml) butter, softened
Salt and freshly ground black pepper
1 teaspoon (5 ml) each minced parsley and chives
6 tablespoons (90 ml) heavy cream
1 tablespoon (15 ml) cognac or Pernod
12 slices firm-textured bread, trimmed of crusts and cut in half diagonally

Purée shrimp, cheese, butter, salt, pepper, parsley, and chives in a blender or a food processor fitted with a steel blade. Add cream and cognac and blend well. Lightly toast bread on one side only. Spread shrimp mixture on the untoasted side, broil just until browned, and cut into triangles.
Makes about 24 appetizers

CHARCOAL-GRILLED SHRIMP

Hot barbecued shrimp are tantalizing, low-calorie morsels for an appetizer plate.

2 pounds (1 kg) large shrimp in
   the shell
1/3 cup (75 ml) safflower oil
1/2 cup (125 ml) fresh lime juice
3 tablespoons (45 ml) dry white wine
   or vermouth
1 tablespoon (15 ml) minced shallots
   or green onions (white part only)
1 garlic clove, minced
1 teaspoon (5 ml) salt
1-1/2 teaspoons (7 ml) minced fresh
   dill weed, or
   1/2 teaspoon (2 ml) crushed dried
   dill weed
Several dashes Tabasco sauce

Place shrimp in a shallow ceramic or glass baking dish. Combine remaining ingredients and pour over shrimp. Cover and chill several hours or overnight. Drain shrimp, reserving marinade. Thread on skewers or place in a wire grill basket. Grill shrimp over hot coals, turning and brushing with reserved marinade, until pink and cooked through, about 8 to 10 minutes. Serve with wooden picks. Let guests shell their own shrimp, or shell before serving, if preferred.
Makes about 30 appetizers

SHRIMP IN BEER

A beach picnic or outdoor party is a good locale for shrimp in the shell. This version is superb.

1 can (12 ounces or 355 ml) beer
1 bay leaf, crumbled
1 dried red chili pepper, split
1 tablespoon (15 ml) mustard seed
Freshly ground black pepper
12 ounces (375 g) medium shrimp in
   the shell
2 tablespoons (30 ml) white wine
   vinegar
1 garlic clove

In a saucepan combine the beer, bay leaf, red pepper, mustard seed, and pepper. Bring to a boil and simmer 5 minutes. Add shrimp and simmer 5 to 6 minutes or until shrimp turn pink. Remove from heat. Place shrimp and liquid in a ceramic or glass bowl, add vinegar and garlic, and let stand half an hour; drain. Chill thoroughly and shell, if desired, before serving.
Makes 6 appetizer servings

MARINATED SQUID

On the terraced balcony of the Royal Danieli in Venice I first encountered squid cooked this way. It was just one of a dozen *antipasti*, including chewy octopus, wine-drenched mussels, tuna with onions, crayfish, and the sweet, succulent Italian crab known as *granceola*.

2 pounds (1 kg) squid
2 tablespoons (30 ml) salt
6 cups (1.5 L) water
1 cup (250 ml) white vinegar
1/4 cup (50 ml) each water and olive
   oil
4 garlic cloves, minced
2 tablespoons (30 ml) minced fresh
   oregano, or
   2 teaspoons (10 ml) crushed dried
   oregano
1/2 teaspoon (2 ml) salt
1/4 teaspoon (1 ml) freshly ground
   black pepper

Clean squid (see page 17) and cut crosswise into 1/2-inch (1 cm) pieces. Add salt to water, bring to a boil, and add squid. Reduce heat, cover, and simmer for 10 to 15 minutes or until squid is tender. Drain, rinse thoroughly in cold water, and then drain again. Combine remaining ingredients in a ceramic or glass dish. Add squid. Cover and marinate several hours in the refrigerator.
Makes 12 appetizer servings

Soups & Stews

FISH SOUP PIRAEUS

I was first introduced to the intricacies of the Greek kitchen by my mother-in-law, who is devoted to her country's cooking. Later, I experienced Greek food firsthand while touring the Greek islands and meeting cousins, aunts, and uncles. This fish soup/stew from Piraeus is first served as either a light fish broth or as a creamy lemon soup enriched with beaten eggs; the poached fish and vegetables follow as a rewarding main course.

1 medium onion, minced
1 stalk celery, minced
1 carrot, minced
1 tablespoon (15 ml) olive oil
4 cups (1 L) water
2 cups (500 ml) Fish Stock, page 115, or clam juice
   cup (250 ml) dry white wine or vermouth
Salt and freshly ground black pepper
One 2-pound (1 kg) piece sea bass, red snapper, rockfish, halibut, or other firm white-fleshed fish, tied in cheesecloth
12 small new potatoes, peeled
1 bunch leeks (white part only), cut in half lengthwise
Parsley-Lemon Sauce or Egg-Lemon Sauce, following
3 tablespoons (45 ml) chopped parsley
1 lemon, cut in wedges

up kettle, sauté onion, carrot in oil until limp. Add ...er, Fish Stock, wine, salt, and pepper and bring to a boil. Add fish and potatoes. Cover and simmer 10 minutes. Add leeks and simmer 10 minutes longer, or until flesh of fish separates when tested with a fork (snip a hole in the cheesecloth to test). Remove fish from broth and place on a heated platter; remove cheesecloth, then remove skin and bones. Spoon potatoes and leeks alongside; keep warm. Add Parsley-Lemon Sauce or Egg-Lemon Sauce to broth, as directed below. Sprinkle fish and vegetables with parsley and accompany with lemon wedges. Serve soup as a first course and follow with fish and vegetables.
Makes 6 servings

PARSLEY-LEMON SAUCE Mix together 2 tablespoons (30 ml) each fresh lemon juice and olive oil with 1 tablespoon (15 ml) finely chopped parsley and stir into the soup.

EGG-LEMON SAUCE Beat together until blended 4 eggs and 1/4 cup (50 ml) fresh lemon juice. Pour 2 cups (500 ml) of the hot prepared broth in a thin stream into the egg mixture, whisking constantly. Return to pan, blending into remaining broth, and stir over low heat until broth is thickened (do not allow to boil).

HONFLEUR FISH STEW

In Normandy, Honfleur with its picturesque bobbing boats is justly famous for this rustic anise-flavored stew.

2 tablespoons (30 ml) butter
1 medium onion, chopped
1 leek, chopped (white part only)
4 cups (1 L) chicken broth
1 cup (250 ml) dry white wine or vermouth
2 medium potatoes, peeled and cut into 1-inch (3 cm) chunks
1 carrot, cut into 1/2-inch (1 cm) slices
1 bay leaf
1/2 teaspoon (2 ml) fennel seeds
1 pound (500 g) boneless chunks of rockfish, red snapper, haddock, halibut or opaka-paka
Salt and freshly ground black pepper to taste

Melt butter in a large saucepan and sauté onion and leek, stirring, until soft. Add chicken broth and wine and bring to a boil. Add potatoes and carrot to the broth along with the bay leaf and fennel. Bring to a boil, cover, and simmer until vegetables are tender, about 20 minutes. Cut fish into small chunks, add to the soup, and cover and simmer about 10 minutes or until flesh of fish separates when tested with a fork. Season with salt and pepper.
Makes 4 to 6 servings

SUQUILLO DE PESCADOR
Spanish Fish Stew

One of the most famous seafood restaurants in Spain is Los Caracoles in Barcelona. Opened in 1835, the restaurant's dark wood-paneled walls are lined with old tiles and paintings of food; garlic braids hang from the ceiling and paella pans line the mantel. A house specialty is Suquillo de Pescador (the word *suquillo* means "little sauce"), a typical dish of the Catalonian fishermen, in which smooth, thick tomato sauce is threaded with amber saffron and crowded with the freshest of fish and shellfish.

1 pound (500 g) rockfish or red snapper fillets
1 pound (500 g) turbot or whiting fillets
2 rock lobster tails
2 large onions, chopped
3 tablespoons (45 ml) olive oil
1 pound (500 g) tomatoes, peeled and chopped, or
   1 can (16 ounces or 450 g) Italian plum tomatoes
1/3 cup (75 ml) ground almonds
3 garlic cloves, minced
1/4 teaspoon (1 ml) ground saffron
1 cup (250 ml) Fish Stock, page 115, or clam juice
2 cups (500 ml) water
1/4 teaspoon (1 ml) salt
6 large shrimp in the shell
6 mussels in the shell (optional)

Cut fish fillets into serving portions and chop each lobster tail, with its shell, crosswise into 4 chunks. Sauté onions in oil until translucent. Add tomatoes and cook until soft. Add almonds, garlic, saffron, and Fish Stock. Simmer 20 to 30 minutes. Purée in a blender or a food processor fitted with a steel blade. Place water and salt in a large pan, add lobster and shrimp, cover, and steam 4 minutes. Add mussels and steam 4 minutes longer. With a slotted spoon, remove shellfish to a large baking dish and arrange fish fillets around shellfish. Cover with sauce. Bake in a preheated 375°F (190°C) oven for 15 minutes or until flesh of fish separates when tested with a fork.
Makes 6 servings

BUGULAMA
Istanbul Fish Stew

Of all the cities I know, Istanbul enchants me most. Exotic, overwhelming, beautifully situated on the sea—it is a jewel. On my visit there, Dr. Kenan Aktan, a Turkish surgeon, graciously presented the charms of the city that only natives know. At a taverna in the fishermen's quarters, ten platefuls of hot and cold appetizers began the meal, including pilaff-stuffed mussels that arrived by basket from a roving street vendor. There were tiny sweet shrimp, drenched in oil and wine vinegar. Crispy batter-dipped smelt were eaten out of hand.

Oval fish croquettes arrived on a bed of Italian parsley. And the classics—puffy, cheese-filled boerek, fried eggplant fingers, and yogurt-cucumber dip—were present, as well. The entrée, *bugulama,* was the star. A mammoth fish stew, it was brought in on a huge platter, the thick fish steaks aswim in a scarlet tomato sauce with spinach, peppers, and parsley.

3 tablespoons (45 ml) olive oil
1 large onion, chopped
1 carrot, chopped
1 red or green bell pepper, seeded and chopped
3 garlic cloves, minced
1 can (6 ounces or 170 g) tomato paste
3/4 cup (175 ml) dry white wine or vermouth
1 cup (250 ml) water
Salt and freshly ground black pepper to taste
1 tablespoon (15 ml) minced fresh basil or,
   1 teaspoon (5 ml) crushed dried basil
1/2 teaspoon (2 ml) ground cumin
2 pounds (1 kg) red snapper fillets, halibut steaks, or other white-fleshed fish fillets or steaks
1 cup (250 ml) shredded spinach leaves
1 large tomato, peeled, seeded, and diced
3 tablespoons (45 ml) chopped Italian parsley

Heat oil in a large Dutch oven or flameproof casserole. Sauté onion, carrot, and pepper until limp. Add garlic, tomato paste, wine, water, salt, pepper, basil, and cumin and simmer 30 minutes or until flavors are blended. Arrange fish fillets in the pan of sauce and bake in a preheated 375°F (190°C) oven for 20 minutes. Stir spinach and chopped tomatoes into the sauce and bake 5 to 10 minutes longer, or until flesh of fish separates when tested with a fork. Sprinkle with parsley.
Makes 6 to 8 servings

MATELOTE OF EEL

Eel has never gained a culinary reputation in the States, though in Europe it is esteemed as a great delicacy. Serve this wine-laced stew as a lusty winter entrée.

1-1/2 pounds (750 g) live eel
2 leeks, sliced (white part only)
12 boiling onions, peeled
3 carrots, thinly sliced
1 turnip, peeled and cut in wedges
   (optional)
1 cup (250 ml) dry white wine or
   vermouth
2 cups (500 ml) chicken broth
1 bay leaf
1-1/2 teaspoons (7 ml) chopped fresh
   thyme, or
   1/2 teaspoon (2 ml) crushed dried
   thyme
2 garlic cloves, minced

1 tablespoon (15 ml) cornstarch mixed
   with
1 tablespoon (15 ml) cold water
1/3 cup (75 ml) heavy cream
Salt and freshly ground black pepper
   to taste
Chopped parsley

Kill the eel, then skin and clean (see page 16). Cut eel into 2-inch (5 cm) crosswise pieces. In a large pan combine leeks, onions, carrots, turnip, wine, broth, bay leaf, thyme, and garlic. Bring to a boil; reduce heat, cover, and simmer 10 minutes. Add eel and simmer gently until flesh separates when tested with a fork, about 15 minutes. With a slotted spoon lift eel and vegetables from poaching liquid and arrange in a 3-quart (1.5 L) casserole. Keep warm. Strain poaching liquid. Bring poaching liquid to a boil and stir in the cornstarch paste; cook, stirring, until thickened. Blend in cream and season with salt and pepper. Pour sauce over fish and vegetables and sprinkle with parsley.
Makes about 6 servings

CACCIUCCO
Italian Seafood Stew

Squid is combined with shrimp, halibut, and sea bass in this Italian dish. To keep the squid tender be sure not to overcook.

8 ounces (250 g) squid
1 small onion, minced
2 garlic cloves, minced
1 tiny dried red chili pepper
1/4 cup (50 ml) olive oil
2 cups (500 ml) water
1/2 cup (125 ml) dry white wine or
   vermouth
1 tablespoon (15 ml) tomato paste
Salt and freshly ground black pepper
   to taste
1 bay leaf
4 ounces (125 g) shrimp, shelled and
   deveined
8 ounces (250 g) each boneless pieces
   of halibut and sea bass or red
   snapper, cut into small chunks
1 minced garlic clove, mixed with
4 tablespoons (60 ml) softened butter
6 slices Italian or French bread

Clean squid (see page 17) and cut into 1/2-inch (1 cm) pieces. In a large soup pot sauté onion, garlic, and pepper in oil until glazed. Add water, wine, tomato paste, salt, pepper, and bay leaf and simmer 10 minutes. Add squid and simmer for 20 minutes. Add shrimp, halibut, and sea bass and simmer 8 to 10 minutes longer or until flesh of fish separates when tested with a fork. Spread garlic butter on bread and toast on both sides under a broiler. Arrange a piece of bread in each of 6 soup bowls and ladle stew over.
Makes 6 servings

SEAFOOD BISQUE

This creamy puréed soup changes character depending on the shellfish that flavors it.

2 cups (500 ml) water
2 medium potatoes, peeled and diced
1 medium onion, chopped
1 leek, chopped (white part only)
1-1/2 teaspoons (7 ml) chopped fresh thyme, or
    1/2 teaspoon (2 ml) crushed dried thyme
1 small garlic clove, minced
Salt and white pepper
1 cup (250 ml) chopped scallops, shrimp, lobster, or crabmeat (preferably raw)
2 cups (500 ml) Fish Stock, page 115, or clam juice
2 egg yolks
1/2 cup (125 ml) heavy cream
Minced parsley

In a large saucepan bring water to a boil, add potatoes, onion, leek, thyme, garlic, salt, and pepper and simmer, covered, for 10 minutes. Add shellfish and simmer 5 minutes longer or until the vegetables are barely tender. Purée the mixture in batches in a blender or a food processor fitted with a steel blade. Return to saucepan, add Fish Stock, and bring to a boil. Beat egg yolks and blend in cream. Stir a small amount of soup into the yolk mixture and return to saucepan. Cook over very low heat, stirring occasionally, until soup is heated through. Ladle into soup bowls and garnish with parsley.
Makes 6 servings

NEW ENGLAND CLAM CHOWDER

West Coast clam enthusiasts claim this chowder as well as Easterners. It was a childhood favorite of mine for Sunday night supper.

3 pounds (1.5 kg) littleneck, cherrystone, butter, or other small hard-shelled clams, or
    2 cans (7 ounces or 196 g each) minced clams
2 ounces (50 g) salt pork or 3 slices bacon, diced
1 large onion, minced
Reserved clam broth
3 medium boiling potatoes, peeled and diced
Salt and freshly ground black pepper
2 cups (500 ml) milk
1/2 cup (125 ml) half-and-half or light cream

Soak clams in salted water for 30 minutes (see page 16). Scrub clams well under cold running water with a stiff-bristled brush. Place them in a kettle with cold water to almost cover, bring to a boil, and simmer gently for about 10 minutes, or until the shells open. Discard any clams that do not open. Strain broth through cheesecloth and reserve. With a small knife, remove clams from shells and clean and chop them. If using canned clams drain, reserving liquid. In a deep saucepan or pot fry salt pork until fat is rendered; do not brown. Add onion and cook until golden. Add reserved broth and potatoes, season with salt and pepper, and cook until tender, about 10 to 15 minutes. Add clams, milk, and cream and heat through. Ladle into soup bowls.
Makes 6 to 8 servings

MANHATTAN CLAM CHOWDER

Unlike New England-style clam chowder, the Manhattan version rests firmly on the tomato, plus assorted vegetables.

3 pounds (1.5 kg) small hard-shelled clams, or
   8 Pismo clams
1/2 cup (125 ml) dry white wine or vermouth
2 ounces (50 g) salt pork or 3 slices bacon, diced
1 large onion, minced
2 tablespoons (30 ml) minced parsley (preferably Italian)
1/2 teaspoon (2 ml) freshly ground black pepper
1/2 bay leaf
1 cup (250 ml) minced celery
1/2 cup (125 ml) minced green bell pepper
4 medium tomatoes, peeled, seeded, and chopped, or
   1 can (16 ounces or 450 g) plum tomatoes, drained and chopped (reserve liquid)
2 cups (500 ml) finely diced peeled potatoes
4 cups (1 L) water
Salt and freshly ground black pepper to taste
1 tablespoon (15 ml) butter
Chopped parsley
Sourdough bread, garlic bread, or oyster crackers

Soak clams in salted water 30 minutes (see page 16). Scrub clams well under cold running water with a stiff-bristled brush. Place in a large kettle with wine, cover, and steam over high heat 5 to 10 minutes, or until shells open; discard any clams that do not open. Remove and drain, reserving 1-1/2 cups (375 ml) broth. With a small knife, remove clams from shells; mince.

In a heavy kettle cook salt pork or bacon with onion, parsley, and pepper until fat is rendered, about 5 minutes. Add bay leaf, celery, and green pepper and sauté 10 minutes. Add reserved clam liquid, reserved liquid from canned tomatoes, potatoes, and water. Cover and simmer 20 minutes, or until potatoes are tender. Add clams and tomatoes and heat through. Season with salt and pepper. Dot with butter and sprinkle with parsley. Serve with bread or oyster crackers.
Makes 4 to 6 servings

CANNED CLAM VARIATION Follow the above recipe, substituting 2 cans (7 ounces or 196 g each) minced clams for the steamed clams. Drain juice from canned clams and add 1 cup (250 ml) clam juice, liquid from tomatoes, potatoes, and water and cook potatoes as directed above.

OYSTER BISQUE

An apropos beginning for a Thanksgiving feast.

1 jar (10 ounces or 284 g) shucked oysters
8 ounces (250 g) spinach
1 small garlic clove, minced
1-1/2 teaspoons (7 ml) chopped fresh tarragon, or
   1/2 teaspoon (2 ml) crushed dried tarragon
2 cups (500 ml) milk
1/2 cup (125 ml) heavy cream
2 egg yolks
2 tablespoons (30 ml) dry sherry
1/4 cup (50 ml) heavy cream, whipped and lightly salted

Wash spinach under cold running water; do not dry. Cook, covered, for 1 minute; drain, squeeze dry, and chop. In a blender or a food processor fitted with a steel blade, purée the oysters, spinach, garlic, and tarragon. Heat milk to simmering and stir in oyster purée. Blend cream with egg yolks and sherry and stir into oyster mixture. Heat thoroughly, stirring constantly. Pour into serving bowls and dollop with whipped cream. If desired, spoon into flameproof bowls, dollop with whipped cream, and place under a broiler until lightly browned.
Makes 6 first-course servings

PUGET SOUND OYSTER STEW

Baby Olympia oysters are magnificent in oyster stew, if you can find them. Without them use small oysters, cut in half.

1 jar (10 ounces or 284 g) shucked
    oysters
2 tablespoons (30 ml) butter
1/2 teaspoon (2 ml) salt
1/4 teaspoon (1 ml) freshly ground
    black pepper
1/2 teaspoon (2 ml) celery salt
1 teaspoon (5 ml) each Worcestershire
    sauce and dry mustard
3 cups (750 ml) milk
3 tablespoons (45 ml) chopped parsley
Crackers (preferably pilot biscuits)

Drain oysters and reserve liquor. Melt butter in saucepan; add oysters and cook until edges curl. Season with salt, pepper, celery salt, Worcestershire, and mustard. Heat milk in a separate pan and bring almost to the boil. Remove from heat and add cooked oysters and reserved oyster liquor. Ladle into bowls and sprinkle with parsley. Serve with crackers.
Makes 4 to 6 servings

CIOPPINO

Live Dungeness crab is the basis of the classic San Francisco seafood stew called *cioppino*. Originated by the Portuguese and Italian fishermen who plied the Bay with their bobbing crab pots, it makes a splendid supper with French or Italian sourdough bread, sweet butter, and a chilled Pinot Blanc or Chardonnay. If live crab is not available, see the variation for *cioppino* made with cooked crab.

1 large live Dungeness crab (about
    2-1/2 pounds or 1.25 kg)
1 carrot, diced
1 leek (white part only), minced
2 green onions, chopped
1 stalk celery, minced
2 tablespoons (30 ml) olive oil
3 garlic cloves, minced
1-1/2 teaspoons (7 ml) each minced
    fresh basil, thyme, and oregano, or
    1/2 teaspoon (2 ml) each crushed
    dried basil, thyme, and oregano
4 medium tomatoes, peeled, seeded,
    and diced, or
    1 can (20 ounces or 560 g) tomato
    purée
1 cup (250 ml) clam juice
1/3 cup (75 ml) dry white wine or
    vermouth
Salt and freshly ground black pepper
    to taste
12 small hard-shelled clams
1 pound (500 g) turbot or red snapper
    fillets, cut into dice
1/4 cup (50 ml) minced parsley

Bring a large kettle of salted water to a boil, then add crab and cook 3 minutes. Remove and plunge into cold water, then drain and cool several minutes. Clean and crack crab as directed on page 15; set aside. In a large soup kettle, sauté carrot, leek, onions, and celery in oil until limp. Add garlic, basil, thyme, oregano, tomatoes, clam juice, and wine and simmer 40 minutes. Season with salt and pepper. Scrub clams well under cold running water with a stiff-bristled brush. Add clams, diced fish, and crab to kettle and simmer 15 minutes. Ladle fish and shellfish along with broth into large bowls and sprinkle with parsley. Offer hot steaming towels to the diners.
Makes 4 to 6 servings

COOKED CRAB VARIATION Remove the crab meat from 1 large cooked, cleaned, and cracked Dungeness crab. Simmer crab shells in 3 cups (750 ml) salted water for 15 minutes to extract flavor. Proceed with the above recipe, adding the strained juices from the crab shells to the kettle along with the herbs, tomato purée, clam juice and wine. Proceed with the recipe, adding crab meat to the kettle to heat through just before serving.

BOUILLABAISSE

This famous fish soup/stew originated in Marseille as a humble dish—the fisherman's salvage of the day's catch, cooked in a broth flavored with typical Mediterranean ingredients. Since then it has evolved into a glorious feast that can contain as many as eight different kinds of fish and half a dozen different kinds of shellfish. The following version calls for fish and shellfish that are usually widely available.

1/2 onion, chopped
1 large leek, chopped (white part only)
3-inch (8 cm) piece celery stalk
3 tablespoons (45 ml) each safflower oil and olive oil
2 tablespoons (30 ml) tomato paste
Tomato Purée, following
8 jumbo shrimp in the shell
2 rock lobster tails (about 6 ounces or 175 g each), split lengthwise
Fish Stock, following
2 cups (500 ml) water
6 to 8 small hard-shelled clams
8 scallops
8 ounces (250 g) each red snapper and sea bass
6 toasted slices of French sourdough bread
Rouille, following

In a large soup kettle, sauté onion, leek, and celery in oil until glazed, about 10 minutes. Add tomato paste and Tomato Purée and cook 10 minutes, stirring; let cool to room temperature. Place the shrimp and lobster tails on top of the vegetables. Add Fish Stock and water, bring to a boil, and simmer exactly 5 minutes. Add clams, scallops, and fish and cover and simmer 5 minutes longer (precise timing is essential so that fish remain firm and intact). Remove fish and shellfish to a heated platter with a slotted spoon and pour broth into a tureen or a large serving bowl. For each serving, spread 2 slices of toasted French bread with Rouille, place in a large soup bowl, and ladle broth over. Add a selection of fish and shellfish to the broth.
Makes 4 servings

TOMATO PURÉE Peel and chop 1 medium tomato and sauté in 1 teaspoon (5 ml) olive oil with 1 minced garlic clove and 1 tablespoon (15 ml) chopped onion several minutes; cover and cook very slowly 45 minutes. Makes 1/3 cup (75 ml). Note: This may be made in quantity and frozen.

FISH STOCK In a large soup pot sauté 1 cup (250 ml) minced onion and 1 chopped leek (white part only) in 1/4 cup (50 ml) each olive oil and peanut oil. Add 4 minced garlic cloves and 1 pound (500 g) seeded and chopped peeled tomatoes. Cook 5 minutes longer. Add 10 cups (2.5 L) water, 1 bay leaf, 1/4 teaspoon (1 ml) each crushed dried thyme and fennel seed, a pinch of saffron and 3 pounds (1.5 kg) lean fish heads, bones, and trimmings. Season with 1 tablespoon (15 ml) salt and freshly ground black pepper to taste. Boil, uncovered, for 30 to 45 minutes. Strain into a saucepan, pressing out all the juices. Makes 4 cups (1 L).

ROUILLE Mince 5 garlic cloves and let stand 1 hour in 2 teaspoons (10 ml) each olive oil and peanut oil. Spoon garlic and oil mixture into a mixing bowl or blender. Add 1 chopped canned pimiento, a dash of Tabasco sauce, 3 egg yolks, 1/2 teaspoon (2 ml) salt and a dash of freshly ground black pepper. Beat with a wire whisk or blend in a blender. Gradually beat in 1-3/4 to 2 cups (375 to 500 ml) of a blend of equal parts olive and peanut oils, adding oil at first drop by drop to create an emulsion, then adding enough to make a thick sauce. Cover and chill thoroughly. Makes about 2 cups (500 ml).

MUSSEL CHOWDER

Utilize steamed mussels for a creamy chowder for a choice midwinter supper.

4 pounds (2 kg) mussels or small hard-shelled clams
1 cup (250 ml) water
1/2 cup (125 ml) dry white wine or vermouth
1 large onion, chopped
1 leek, chopped (white part only)
1 garlic clove, minced
3 tablespoons (45 ml) butter
4 ounces (125 g) mushrooms
1-1/2 cups (375 ml) chicken broth
1-1/2 teaspoons (7 ml) chopped fresh thyme, or
    1/2 teaspoon (2 ml) crushed dried thyme
1 cup (250 ml) light cream
3 tablespoons (45 ml) dry sherry

Soak mussels in salted water for 30 minutes (see page 16), then scrub well under cold running water with a stiff-bristled brush; cut off beards. Place in a large kettle with water and wine, cover, and steam 5 to 10 minutes, or until shells open; discard any mussels that do not open. Reserve 1-1/2 cups (375 ml) of the broth. Remove mussels from shells and set aside. In a large kettle, sauté onion, leek, and garlic in butter until onion is soft, stirring occasionally. Add mushrooms and sauté 1 minute. Add chicken broth, mussel broth, and thyme and bring to a boil. Cover and simmer 15 minutes. Stir in cream and mussels and heat through. Add sherry.
Makes 6 servings

OCTOPUS STEW

Oriental and Mediterranean cooks consider octopus a delicacy, but in the States it is often bypassed. Here is a Provençal octopus stew.

1 pound (500 g) octopus
2 tablespoons (30 ml) olive oil
2 green onions, chopped
1 medium onion, chopped
2 large tomatoes, peeled, seeded, and diced
1 tablespoon (15 ml) chopped parsley
2 garlic cloves, minced
1 teaspoon (5 ml) minced fresh thyme, or
    1/4 teaspoon (1 ml) crushed dried thyme
1 teaspoon (5 ml) minced fresh basil, or
    1/4 teaspoon (1 ml) crushed dried basil or fennel
3/4 cup (175 ml) dry white wine or vermouth
Salt and freshly ground black pepper to taste
French bread

Slit open head cavity of octopus and discard interior. Cut away and discard beak. Wash octopus well under cold running water. Separate head and tentacles; drop into a large kettle filled with boiling salted water to cover. Cover and simmer 30 minutes, or until skin can be peeled and stripped away from flesh. Let octopus cool in its broth, then drain, peel off skin, and cut meat into dice. In a large frying pan heat oil and add both kinds of onion, tomatoes, parsley, garlic, thyme, and basil. Cook and stir until vegetables are soft. Add octopus and wine and stir to blend; season with salt and pepper. Pour into a 6-cup (1.5 L) casserole, cover, and bake in a preheated 325°F (160°C) oven for 2 hours, stirring once or twice. Serve hot, accompanied with French bread.
Makes 4 servings

Salads

GREEK AVGOLEMONO FISH SALAD

The White Tower, a sophisticated London restaurant, specializes in gifted Greek cuisine. This stunning fish platter—done with mackerel there—is an outstanding first course from their cold table.

2-1/2 pounds (1.25 kg) halibut or swordfish steaks, cut about 1 inch (3 cm) thick
4 each whole allspice and peppercorns
2 slices lemon
1 carrot, cut in chunks
1 onion, cut in chunks
1/2 teaspoon (2 ml) salt
2 cups (500 ml) water
1 cucumber, peeled and sliced
1/2 cup (125 ml) cherry tomatoes, halved
12 Greek olives
Parsley or fresh coriander sprigs
Avgolemono Sauce, following
8 large shrimp, cooked, shelled, and deveined

Place fish steaks in a large frying pan. Add allspice, peppercorns, lemons, carrot, onion, salt, and water. Bring to a boil, reduce heat, cover, and simmer until flesh of fish separates when tested with a fork, about 10 minutes. Transfer fish to a serving platter, reserving poaching liquid. Arrange the steaks in a single layer; cover and chill. Strain poaching liquid and reserve. To serve, arrange fish steaks in a row on a platter. Arrange cucumber slices and tomato halves around fish. Tuck in olives and parsley. Spoon Avgolemono Sauce over fish and garnish with shrimp.
Makes about 8 servings

AVGOLEMONO SAUCE In the top of a double boiler over high heat boil down the reserved poaching juices until reduced to 3/4 cup (175 ml). Beat 3 egg yolks until light and beat in 1-1/2 tablespoons (25 ml) lemon juice. Gradually stir hot poaching liquid into the egg mixture. Return to top of double boiler and place over hot (not boiling) water. Stirring, cook until sauce is thickened. Let cool, then chill thoroughly. Blend in 1 cup (250 ml) sour cream, or 1/2 cup (125 ml) sour cream and 1/2 cup (125 ml) yogurt. Chill again. Makes about 2 cups (500 ml).

BALI HAI FISH SALAD

A specialty of Tahiti is marinated fish salad with coconut milk. This version is from the Bali Hai Hotel.

1 coconut
2 pounds (1 kg) mahi-mahi or tuna fillets
Juice of 8 limes (about 1 cup or 250 ml lime juice)
2 cups (500 ml) chopped mixed vegetables such as tomatoes, white onions, cucumbers, and carrots
1 clove garlic, minced
Salt and freshly ground black pepper

Pierce one eye of coconut with an ice pick; drain off the liquid and reserve. Crack open the shell, cut out meat, then peel; purée in a blender with enough hot water to make a smooth sauce; strain. Dice fish and place in a ceramic or glass bowl. Pour lime juice over and let stand for 15 minutes. Pour off about two-thirds of the lime juice and mix in chopped vegetables, stirring lightly with a fork. Season with garlic, salt, and pepper. Add coconut liquid. Chill thoroughly before serving.
Makes about 8 servings

HERRING SALAD

Fish salad is a Swedish classic for any smorgasbord table. It is traditionally served for lunch on Christmas Eve day.

1 salt herring, or
    2 jars (5 ounces or 140 g each)
    pickled herring
1-1/2 cups (375 ml) each diced
    pickled beets and diced peeled
    boiled potatoes
1 red apple, cored and diced
1/4 cup (50 ml) each chopped red
    onion and diced gherkin pickles
1/4 cup (50 ml) white vinegar
2 tablespoons (30 ml) water
2 tablespoons (30 ml) sugar
Freshly ground black pepper
1/4 cup (50 ml) heavy cream,
    whipped, or sour cream
Salad greens
2 hard-cooked eggs, sliced or quartered
Parsley sprigs

Remove head and skin of herring and soak herring overnight in cold water. Drain and split; remove and discard bones; dice. If using pickled herring, drain and dice. Mix gently with beets, potatoes, apple, onion, and pickles. Mix together vinegar, water, sugar, and pepper and add to the herring mixture.

Mix in cream. Pack into a mold, such as a charlotte mold, that has been rinsed out in cold water. Cover and chill several hours. Unmold on greens and garnish with eggs and parsley.
Makes 6 servings

LOMI LOMI SALMON

This is a Hawaiian version of pickled salmon. Serve as an appealing appetizer salad or a first course.

1-1/2 pounds (750 g) salmon fillets,
    skinned
Coarse rock salt
2 large tomatoes, peeled, seeded, and
    diced
1 small white onion, chopped
Juice of 6 limes (about 3/4 cup or
    175 ml lime juice)
1/2 teaspoon (2 ml) salt
1 teaspoon (5 ml) sugar
1/2 teaspoon (2 ml) white pepper
Salad greens or avocado halves

Lay the salmon fillets in a ceramic or glass dish on a bed of rock salt. Cover with more rock salt. Cover and refrigerate overnight or up to 2 days. Drain and rinse off the salt. Dice the fish. Combine with the tomatoes and onions in a bowl. Pour lime juice over and season with salt, sugar, and pepper. Mix together well and chill for 4 to 6 hours or overnight before serving on salad greens or in avocado halves.
Makes 6 to 8 first-course servings

TRINIDAD SALT COD SALAD

The humble salt cod is the basis of traditional dishes in many cuisines, including French, Italian, Portuguese, and Chinese. In this unusual Caribbean salad, salt cod is transformed into a refreshing hot-weather entrée.

1 pound (500 g) salt cod
8 ounces (250 g) cooked small shrimp
1/4 cup (50 ml) fresh lemon juice
1/2 cup (125 ml) olive oil
1/2 teaspoon (2 ml) salt
1/4 teaspoon (1 ml) white pepper
Dash Tabasco sauce
1 teaspoon (5 ml) chopped fresh
    oregano, or
    1/4 teaspoon (1 ml) crushed dried
    oregano
1 red or green bell pepper, seeded and
    chopped
1 small red onion, chopped
1/2 cup (125 ml) whole pitted green
    olives
1 celery heart, sliced
1 cup (250 ml) cherry tomatoes,
    halved
Lettuce leaves
1 avocado, peeled and sliced

Soak salt cod overnight in cold water to cover, changing water twice. Drain and place in a saucepan. Add cold water to cover and bring to a boil. Simmer 20 minutes; drain. Skin, bone, and flake fish. Place fish in a mixing bowl and allow to cool. Add shrimp to the fish. Mix together lemon juice and

A WEST COAST
FISHERIES DEVELOPMENT
FOUNDATION RECIPE

Shrimp Creole

1-1/2 pounds Tiny Pacific Shrimp
3 tablespoons butter
1 cup coarsely chopped onion
1 cup coarsely chopped green pepper
1 cup coarsely chopped zucchini or celery
2 cloves garlic, finely minced
4 large tomatoes, peeled and chopped
1 can (8 ounces) tomato sauce

1/2 teaspoon black pepper
2 teaspoons shredded fresh lemon rind
3 whole cloves
1 bay leaf
1/2 teaspoon dried thyme
1/2 teaspoon honey
3 tablespoons finely minced fresh parsley

Rinse shrimp with cold water; pat dry with paper towels. Set aside. In large saucepan, over medium heat, melt butter. Add onion, green pepper and zucchini; sauté until tender but not brown. Add garlic and tomatoes; bring to boil. Reduce heat. Add tomato sauce, pepper, lemon rind, cloves, bay leaf, thyme and honey. Simmer for 15-20 minutes, stirring frequently. Stir in shrimp; heat thoroughly. Serve over hot rice. Garnish with parsley. Makes 6 servings.

... slices, tomato wedges, cucumber slices, egg slices, and mushrooms. Pass Green Mayonnaise.
Makes 6 servings

CRAB LOUIS

Crab Louis, laden with sweet, just-cooked Dungeness crab from the Oregon seashore, was one of my childhood treats. A famous West Coast salad, its origin remains a mystery, although Solari's Grill in San Francisco was one of the first restaurants to serve it around 1911. Louis Dressing will also enhance a salad plate of tiny shrimp, king crab, or lobster.

1 head iceberg lettuce
1 pound (500 g) flaked cooked crab
   meat
4 cracked cooked crab legs (optional)
4 tomatoes, cut in wedges
4 hard-cooked eggs, quartered
Pitted black olives, sliced dill pickle,
   and white asparagus spears
   (optional)
Louis Dressing, following

For each salad arrange 2 or 3 outer leaves of lettuce on a large plate. Shred inner leaves and mound in the center. Mound crab meat on the shredded lettuce, arranging legs on top. Garnish with tomato wedges, egg quarters, and, if desired, olives, sliced pickle, and asparagus spears. Pass or spoon over Louis Dressing.
Makes 4 servings

LOUIS DRESSING Mix together 3/4 cup (175 ml) mayonnaise, 3 tablespoons (45 ml) chili sauce, 2 teaspoons (10 ml) fresh lemon juice and 3 drops

Angostura bitters. Whip 1/4 cup (50 ml) heavy cream and fold in. Chill. Makes about 1-1/2 cups (375 ml) dressing, or enough for 4 to 6 servings.

CRAB AND GREEN SALAD HAWAIIAN

Crab meat blends beautifully with avocado and papaya in a main-course salad for a luncheon or a summer supper.

1 head romaine lettuce
1 bunch watercress
1 small papaya, peeled and sliced
1 avocado, peeled and sliced
12 ounces (375 g) flaked cooked crab
   meat or lobster meat, or small
   cooked shrimp
Chili Dressing, following

Tear romaine into bite-sized pieces, making about 4 cups (1 L) torn greens, and place in a salad bowl. Pull leaves from watercress and pile on top. Arrange papaya and avocado slices in a pinwheel on top of the greens. Mound crab in the center. Pour Chili Dressing over and mix at the table.
Makes 4 entrée servings

CHILI DRESSING Mix together 1/3 cup (75 ml) olive oil, 3 tablespoons (45 ml) each tarragon-flavored white wine vinegar and chili sauce, and salt and white pepper to taste. Add a dash of Tabasco sauce or Angostura bitters. Cover and chill thoroughly.

BLUE CHEESE MOLD WITH SEAFOOD

A creamy cheese mold showered with chives and ringed with seafood and relishes.

1 envelope (1 tablespoon or 15 ml)
    unflavored gelatin
1/4 cup (50 ml) cold water
4 ounces (125 g) blue cheese
1/2 cup (125 ml) sour cream (half
    yogurt, if desired)
1-1/2 tablespoons (25 ml) fresh lemon
    juice
1/4 teaspoon salt
Few drops Tabasco sauce
1 cup (250 ml) heavy cream
1 tablespoon (15 ml) chopped chives
Butter lettuce leaves
1 pound (500 g) cooked small shrimp
    or flaked cooked crab meat, or
    8 ounces (225 g) each cooked small
    shrimp and flaked cooked crab meat
1 basket cherry tomatoes, halved
1 English cucumber, thinly sliced
3 hard-cooked eggs, quartered
Pitted black olives

Sprinkle gelatin into cold water and let stand until softened; dissolve over hot water. Cream cheese until soft and blend in sour cream, lemon juice, salt, and Tabasco. Mix in the liquid gelatin and beat until smooth. Whip cream until stiff and fold in. Turn into an oiled 4-cup (1 L) charlotte mold or other small mold and chill until firm. Line a platter with lettuce leaves. Dip mold in a pan of hot water and turn out onto platter. Surround with shrimp, tomatoes, cucumber, eggs, and olives.
Makes 6 servings

FINNISH SHRIMP AND VEGETABLE PLATTER

On an overnight sailing from Helsinki to Stockholm, a stunning smorgasbord was set out in the contemporary dining saloon. This was just one of four dozen selections for the midnight feast. Here shrimp substitutes for the crayfish that typically grace this salad platter. This dish is ideal for a midday party luncheon or a late supper.

1 pound (500 g) asparagus, cooked
    and chilled
6 ounces (175 g) mushrooms, sliced
1/3 cup (75 ml) olive or safflower oil
2 tablespoons (30 ml) tarragon-
    flavored white wine vinegar
1/4 teaspoon (1 ml) each salt and
    dry mustard
Butter lettuce
1 pound (500 g) small or medium
    shrimp, cooked, shelled and
    deveined, or crayfish, cooked and
    shelled
1 cucumber, sliced
2 tomatoes, cut in wedges
Sour Cream Caper Dressing, following

Place asparagus and mushrooms in separate bowls. Combine oil, vinegar, salt, and mustard and pour over, mixing each lightly. Cover and chill 1 hour. Arrange greens on a platter and mound shrimp in the center. Surround with clusters of asparagus spears, mushrooms, cucumber slices, and tomato wedges. Accompany with Sour Cream Caper Dressing.
Makes 6 entrée servings

SOUR CREAM CAPER DRESSING
Mix together 6 tablespoons (90 ml) each mayonnaise and sour cream, 1 tablespoon (15 ml) white wine vinegar, 2 teaspoons (10 ml) anchovy paste, 2 tablespoons (30 ml) each chopped parsley and capers, and salt and white pepper to taste. Cover and chill thoroughly.

SHRIMP AND MUSHROOM SALAD

A Danish discovery: fresh mushrooms and tiny shrimp in a green salad with a Danish blue cheese dressing. Exotic enoki, or snow, mushrooms are charming here.

1 head butter lettuce
1 head red leaf lettuce
4 ounces (125 g) medium mushrooms,
    sliced
12 cherry tomatoes, halved
1 cup (250 ml) alfalfa sprouts
4 ounces (125 g) small cooked shrimp
Danish Blue Cheese Dressing, following

Tear both heads of lettuce into bite-sized pieces and place in a salad bowl. Add mushrooms, tomatoes, sprouts, and shrimp to greens. Spoon dressing over and mix well.
Makes 6 first-course servings

DANISH BLUE CHEESE DRESSING
Place 2 to 3 ounces (50 to 75 g) blue cheese in a small bowl and mash with a fork. Mix in 3 tablespoons (45 ml) white wine vinegar, 2 teaspoons (10 ml) fresh lemon juice, 1/2 teaspoon (2 ml) anchovy paste, 1 teaspoon (5 ml) Dijon-style mustard, 1/4 teaspoon (1 ml) salt, and 1 garlic clove, mashed. Blend in 6 tablespoons (90 ml) olive oil. Cover and chill thoroughly.

SHRIMP-STUFFED ARTICHOKES

Whole boiled artichokes make handsome cases for shrimp. Nothing could be simpler or more elegant for a luncheon or late supper.

4 large artichokes
1 tablespoon (15 ml) olive oil
Butter lettuce leaves
Tarragon Dressing, following, or
    Aioli, page 122, or Green Mayonnaise, page 119
12 ounces (375 g) cooked small shrimp
Cherry tomatoes (optional)

Slice off the top third of each artichoke. Break off all coarse outer bottom leaves. Clip off tops of remaining leaves with scissors. Slice off stem to make a flat base. Drop into a large amount of salted boiling water, add olive oil, and simmer for 30 to 40 minutes, depending on the size. Drain upside down until cool. With a spoon, carefully remove the choke and enough center leaves to make a generous hollow in each artichoke. Chill thoroughly. To serve, arrange butter lettuce on individual plates. Place artichokes on top, spoon a small amount of Tarragon Dressing in each and spoon shrimp on top. If desired, garnish with cherry tomatoes.
Makes 4 servings

TARRAGON DRESSING Mix together 1/2 cup (125 ml) mayonnaise, 1/3 cup (75 ml) sour cream, 2 tablespoons (30 ml) fresh lemon juice, 1 teaspoon (5 ml) grated lemon peel, 1-1/2 teaspoons (7 ml) chopped fresh tarragon or 1/2 teaspoon (2 ml) crushed dried tarragon, and 1/4 teaspoon (1 ml) each salt and Dijon-style mustard. Cover and chill.

ITALIAN SQUID SALAD

Squid is one of the most economical seafoods. Here it is in a cool salad, just as I first tried it at an Alemagna food shop in Rome.

2 pounds (1 kg) small squid
1/4 cup (50 ml) olive oil
1-1/2 tablespoons (25 ml) fresh lemon juice
2 teaspoons (10 ml) chopped fresh mint
2 tablespoons (30 ml) minced parsley
Salt, freshly ground black pepper, and celery salt to taste
2 celery hearts, thinly sliced
2 green onions, chopped
1/2 cup (125 ml) mayonnaise
2 tablespoons (30 ml) white wine vinegar
2 teaspoons (10 ml) anchovy paste
Leaf lettuce leaves
2 or 3 hard-cooked eggs
2 or 3 ripe tomatoes

Clean the squid (see page 17). Bring a large pot of salted water to a rapid boil. Add squid and boil until tender, about 20 minutes. Drain. Let cool and dice. Mix together olive oil, lemon juice, mint, parsley, salt, pepper, and celery salt. Add squid and let marinate for several hours. Just before serving mix in celery and onions. Combine mayonnaise, vinegar, and anchovy paste and stir in. Arrange lettuce leaves on a platter and spoon squid mixture in the center. Ring with wedges of eggs and tomatoes.
Makes about 6 servings

Casseroles & Gratins

MUSSELS AU BRESSANE

A tiny French bistro in Grenoble—Auberge Bressane—more than merits its Michelin star with a first-course specialty of mussels swimming in a winey Roquefort cheese sauce. The idea adapts easily to scallops or shrimp instead (see variation).

5 pounds (2.5 kg) mussels
2 cups (500 ml) water
1 shallot or green onion (white part only), chopped
1 garlic clove, minced
2 tablespoons (30 ml) butter
3 tablespoons (45 ml) brandy or cognac
1/2 cup (125 ml) dry white wine or vermouth
1/4 cup (50 ml) heavy cream
1 tablespoon (15 ml) cornstarch blended with
1 tablespoon (15 ml) cold water
3 ounces (75 g) Roquefort or blue cheese
2 tablespoons (30 ml) chopped parsley

Soak mussels for 30 minutes in salted water (see page 16). Scrub mussels well under cold running water with a stiff-bristled brush; cut off beards. Place mussels in a large kettle with water. Cover and steam over high heat 5 to 10 minutes, or until shells open; discard any mussels that do not open. Remove mussels from pan with a slotted spoon, then remove mussels from shells with a small knife. Measure and reserve 1/2 cup (125 ml) mussel broth. In a large frying pan sauté shallot and garlic in butter until soft. Add mussels and sauté lightly. Add brandy, ignite, and cook, shaking pan until flames die out. Remove mussels with a slotted spoon and keep warm. Add to the pan the reserved broth, wine, and cream and bring to a boil. Let cook down slightly. Stir in cornstarch paste and, stirring, cook until thickened. Crumble cheese and mix in, heating just until cheese melts. Return mussels to the pan and heat through. Spoon into hot ramekins and sprinkle with parsley.
Makes 4 servings

VARIATION Substitute scallops or medium shrimp for the steamed mussels. If using sea scallops, cut them in quarters; if using shrimp, shell and devein, then butterfly as directed on page 17. Substitute 1/2 cup (125 ml) clam juice for the mussel broth.

CRAB AND AVOCADO MOUSSELINE

These individual party entrées belong to a party occasion. Serve with fresh asparagus and croissants.

8 ounces (250 g) mushrooms, sliced
3 tablespoons (45 ml) butter
1 garlic clove, minced
2 teaspoons (10 ml) fresh lemon juice
1 pound (500 g) flaked cooked crab meat or cooked small shrimp
2 tablespoons (30 ml) brandy or cognac
1 avocado, peeled and diced
Mousseline Sauce, page 125

In a large frying pan sauté mushrooms in butter with garlic and lemon juice for 1 minute. Add crab meat and shake pan, tossing to coat. Add brandy, ignite, and let juices cook down. Remove from heat and mix in avocado. Spoon into buttered clam shells or small ramekins. Spoon Mousseline Sauce over and broil until lightly browned.
Makes 4 servings

CRAB AND ARTICHOKE CASSEROLE

For a delectable luncheon, pair crab casserole with a green salad pinwheeled with pink grapefruit sections and avocado slices. Pass flaky croissants and sweet butter and pour a crisp Pinot Blanc or Muscadet.

18 baby artichokes, trimmed of bases and outer leaves, or
2 packages (9 ounces or 252 g each) frozen artichoke hearts
4 ounces (125 g) mushrooms
5 tablespoons (75 ml) butter
4 tablespoons (60 ml) flour
3/4 cup (175 ml) each milk and half-and-half
1/4 cup (50 ml) dry sherry
Salt and freshly ground black pepper to taste
2 teaspoons (10 ml) Worcestershire sauce
4 ounces (125 g) Gruyère or Jarlsberg cheese, shredded (about 1 cup or 250 ml)
1 pound (500 g) flaked cooked crab meat or lobster meat or small cooked shrimp, or a combination of these seafoods

Cook artichoke hearts in boiling salted water, allowing 20 to 25 minutes for the fresh ones and 5 to 7 minutes for frozen; drain. Leave mushrooms whole if small or slice larger ones, and sauté in 1 tablespoon (15 ml) of the butter until glazed, about 1 minute. Melt remaining 4 tablespoons (60 ml) butter in a saucepan, stir in flour, and cook 2 minutes, stirring. Gradually mix in milk and cream, adding a small amount at a time, and cook until thickened, stirring constantly. Add sherry and season with salt, pepper, and Worcestershire. Mix in 1/2 cup (125 ml) of the cheese. Arrange artichoke hearts in a buttered 8-cup (2 L) baking dish. Scatter mushrooms and seafood over. Spoon cheese sauce over and sprinkle with remaining cheese. Bake in a preheated 375°F (190°C) oven for 20 to 25 minutes, or until heated through and bubbly.
Makes 4 to 6 servings

CRAB-STUFFED PAPAYA TAHAITIAN

Papaya half-shells make exotic bowls for sherry-seasoned crab. Place a blossom or two on the serving plate to lend a tropical touch.

2 tablespoons (30 ml) butter
1 shallot or green onion (white part only), chopped
2 tablespoons (30 ml) flour
3/4 cup (175 ml) milk
1/4 cup (50 ml) dry sherry
Salt and white pepper to taste
1 teaspoon (5 ml) Worcestershire sauce
1 teaspoon (5 ml) grated lemon peel
1 pound (500 g) flaked cooked crab meat or lobster meat, or cooked small shrimp
1 ounce (25 g) Gruyère or Jarlsberg cheese, shredded (about 1/4 cup or 50 ml)
3 small ripe papayas, halved and seeded
1-1/2 tablespoons (25 ml) fresh lime or lemon juice
Toasted coconut, slivered almonds, or chopped macadamia nuts

Melt butter in a saucepan and sauté shallot until soft. Blend in flour and cook 2 minutes. Gradually stir in milk and sherry and cook until thickened. Season with salt, pepper, Worcestershire, and lemon peel. Mix in seafood and cheese. Place the papaya shells in a baking pan and sprinkle with lime juice. Spoon the crab into the cavity. Bake in a preheated 350°F (180°C) oven for 10 to 15 minutes or until heated through. Place on a serving plate and garnish with coconut.
Makes 6 servings

CRAB ENCHILADAS

For a party luncheon or supper this Mexican-style entrée is easily made in advance, ready for last-minute baking. Accompany with a platter of sliced fresh fruit such as watermelon, pineapple, papaya, and honeydew.

Corn or safflower oil for frying
12 corn tortillas
1-1/2 pounds (750 g) flaked cooked
    crab meat
2 bunches green onions, chopped
2 tablespoons (30 ml) butter
Tomatillo Sauce, page 118
12 ounces (325) Monterey Jack
    cheese, shredded (about 3 cups or
    375 ml)
1 can (5-3/4 ounces or 161 g) pitted
    jumbo black olives
1 large avocado, peeled and sliced
1 large tomato, cut into wedges
Sour Cream Sauce, following

Heat 1/8 inch (3 mm) oil in a large frying pan and fry tortillas until lightly browned on the edges; drain on absorbent paper. Sauté onions in butter until soft. Spread about 1/4 cup (50 ml) of the crab meat in a ribbon on each tortilla, sprinkle with onions and about 1 tablespoon (15 ml) of the Tomatillo Sauce and roll up. Arrange seam side down in a greased baking dish. Lightly spoon Tomatillo Sauce over and sprinkle with cheese. Bake in a preheated 400°F (210°C) oven for 15 minutes, or until heated through. Garnish with olives. Arrange avocado slices and tomato wedges on top. Pass the Sour Cream Sauce.
Makes 6 servings

SOUR CREAM SAUCE Mix together 1 cup (250 ml) sour cream, 1 tablespoon (15 ml) chopped fresh coriander or parsley, 1/4 teaspoon (1 ml) salt, a small minced garlic clove, and 1 chopped green onion.

DEVILED BLUE CRAB

Water chestnuts lend a delightful crunch to deviled crab. Serve as a first course or as a luncheon or supper entrée.

8 to 10 live hard-shell blue crabs
    (about 6 ounces or 175 g each), or
    1 pound (500 g) flaked cooked
    crab meat
1 shallot or green onion (white part
    only), chopped

2 tablespoons (30 ml) butter
2 tablespoons (30 ml) flour
1 cup (250 ml) hot rich milk (part
    half-and-half or heavy cream)
1/2 teaspoon (2 ml) each salt and dry
    mustard
1 teaspoon (5 ml) Worcestershire sauce
2 teaspoons (10 ml) fresh lemon juice
Dash Tabasco sauce
1/2 cup (125 ml) sliced canned water
    chestnuts
2 tablespoons (30 ml) chopped
    parsley
2 green onions, chopped
2 pimientos, chopped (optional)
2 hard-cooked eggs, chopped
1/2 cup (125 ml) fresh bread crumbs
    mixed with
2 tablespoons (30 ml) melted butter

Cook, clean, and crack crabs (see page 16) and remove crab meat; reserve 6 crab shells. In a saucepan sauté shallot in butter, blend in flour, and cook and stir 2 minutes; do not let flour brown. Gradually stir in milk and season with salt, mustard, and Worcestershire; cook until thickened, stirring occasionally. Mix in lemon juice and Tabasco. Mix in water chestnuts, parsley, onion, pimientos, eggs, and crab meat. Turn into 6 buttered crab or scallop shells or ramekins. Sprinkle with crumbs. Bake in a preheated 400°F (210°C) oven for 15 minutes or until browned.
Makes 6 servings

POLYNESIAN LOBSTER TAILS

Chutney and macadamia nuts are exotic additions to deviled lobster tails.

6 rock lobster tails (about 4 ounces or
    125 g each)
4 tablespoons (60 ml) butter
2 teaspoons (10 ml) dry mustard
1/2 teaspoon (2 ml) Worcestershire
    sauce
1 bay leaf
Juice of 1 lime
3 tablespoons (45 ml) soft bread
    crumbs
2 medium tomatoes, peeled, seeded,
    and chopped
1/4 cup (50 ml) chutney, diced
2 tablespoons (30 ml) dry sherry
3 tablespoons (45 ml) chopped
    unsalted macadamia nuts or cashews
Grated Parmesan cheese

Drop lobster tails into boiling salted water. When water reboils, cook tails for 4 minutes. Drain immediately, plunge into cold water, and drain again. With a small pair of scissors, cut along both sides of the white underside of the shell and pull it off. Remove meat from shells, reserving shells. Cut meat into cubes. In a large frying pan melt butter and add mustard, Worcestershire, bay leaf, and lime juice, then add bread crumbs, lobster, tomatoes, chutney, sherry, and nuts. Heat mixture through and stuff into shells. Sprinkle lightly with cheese and brown under a broiler.
Makes 6 servings

DEVILED CLAMS PISMO BEACH

This is a favorite clam-digging recipe. Garlic-buttered sourdough bread and a Caesar salad are prime accompaniments, along with a crisp dry white wine—a Pinot Blanc or Johannisberg Riesling.

12 Pismo clams, or
    5 pounds (2.5 kg) small hard-shelled
    clams
1 small onion, minced
1/3 cup (75 ml) minced celery heart
2 tablespoons (30 ml) butter
1 cup (250 ml) toasted French bread
    crumbs
2 eggs
1 cup (250 ml) half-and-half or heavy
    cream
2 teaspoons (10 ml) Dijon-style
    mustard
Dash each Tabasco and Worcestershire
    sauce
3 tablespoons (45 ml) dry white wine
    or vermouth
1 ounce (25 g) prosciutto or ham,
    minced
2 ounces (50 g) Parmesan or Romano
    cheese, grated (about 1/2 cup or
    125 ml)
Salt and white pepper to taste

Soak clams in salted water 30 minutes (see page 16). Scrub clams thoroughly under cold running water with a stiff-bristled brush. Open clams with a small knife, remove meat, and grind in a food grinder; set aside. Sauté onion and celery in butter until soft. Mix in bread crumbs and sauté lightly; set aside. Beat eggs and mix in cream, mustard, Tabasco, Worcestershire sauce, wine, prosciutto, half of the cheese, the vegetable mixture, clams, and salt and pepper. Spoon into 6 buttered Pismo clam shells or scallop shells and sprinkle with remaining cheese. Bake in a preheated 375°F (190°C) oven for 15 minutes or until golden brown.
Makes 6 servings

SCALLOPED OYSTERS

A traditional oyster dish from the American South.

3 jars (10 ounces or 284 g each)
    shucked oysters
Milk or half-and-half
4 tablespoons (60 ml) butter
1 medium onion, chopped
1/2 medium green bell pepper, seeded
    and chopped
1/4 cup (50 ml) flour
1/2 teaspoon (2 ml) each salt, paprika,
    and dry mustard
1/4 teaspoon (1 ml) white pepper
1 garlic clove, minced
1 tablespoon (15 ml) fresh lemon
    juice
2 teaspoons (10 ml) Worcestershire
    sauce
1 cup (250 ml) cracker crumbs

Drain oysters, reserving liquor. Add enough milk to the reserved liquor to make 2 cups (500 ml). In a small saucepan, bring almost to a simmer and keep warm. In a large frying pan melt butter, add onion and green pepper and sauté a few minutes. Stir in flour and cook and stir 2 minutes; do not let flour brown. Season with salt, paprika, mustard, pepper, and garlic. Add milk-oyster liquor mixture and stir and cook until thickened. Add lemon juice, Worcestershire sauce, and oysters. Spoon into a buttered casserole or individual ramekins or casseroles. Sprinkle with crumbs. Bake in a preheated 400°F (210°C) oven for 20 minutes, or until heated through and lightly browned.
Makes 6 to 8 servings

SEAFOOD GRATINÉE

An exquisite dish for a late supper or a special luncheon. The ramekins may be assembled in advance, ready for last-minute heating.

1 pound (500 g) mushrooms, sliced
6 tablespoons (90 ml) butter
Salt and white pepper
1-1/2 teaspoons (7 ml) chopped fresh
    tarragon, or
    1/2 teaspoon (2 ml) crushed dried
    tarragon
3 tablespoons (45 ml) sherry
1 pound (500 g) diced cooked lobster
    meat, flaked cooked crab meat, or
    cooked small shrimp
2 tablespoons (30 ml) flour
1 cup (250 ml) half-and-half or light
    cream
Salt and white pepper to taste
2 tablespoons (30 ml) brandy or
    cognac
1 ounce (25 g) Parmesan cheese,
    grated (about 1/4 cup or 50 ml)
1 ounce (25 g) Gruyère or Jarlsberg
    cheese, shredded (about 1/4 cup
    or 50 ml)

In a large frying pan sauté mushrooms in 2 tablespoons (30 ml) of the butter for about 1 minute. Season with salt, pepper, and tarragon. Add 1 tablespoon (15 ml) of the sherry and spoon into 4 buttered ramekins or baking dishes. Heat 1-1/2 tablespoons (25 ml) butter, add lobster, and toss to coat and heat lightly. Spoon over mushrooms. In a small saucepan melt 2 tablespoons (30 ml) of the butter, stir in flour, and cook and stir 2 minutes; do not let flour brown. Add cream, bring to a boil, and cook until thickened, stirring occasionally. Season with salt, pepper, the remaining 2 tablespoons (30 ml) sherry, and the brandy and spoon over lobster. Sprinkle with the cheeses. Dot with remaining butter. Place under a broiler until golden brown.
Makes 4 servings

Specialty Dishes

GEFILTE FISH

In the Jewish tradition fish dumplings are a holiday specialty, along with chicken soup and challah. This version comes from one of my former students.

2 pounds (1 kg) whitefish, carp, or
 pike
4 cups (1 L) water
2 onions, sliced
2 carrots, sliced
2-1/2 teaspoons (12 ml) sugar
Salt and white pepper
4 eggs
2 teaspoons (10 ml) salt
1 teaspoon (15 ml) white pepper
2 carrots, grated
2 onions, grated
2 tablespoons (30 ml) matzo meal
Horseradish sauce

Remove skin and bones from fish. Cut fish into chunks and put through a food grinder or grind in batches in a food processor fitted with a steel blade. In a large saucepan combine water, sliced onions and carrots, 2 teaspoons (10 ml) of the sugar, salt, and pepper. Bring to a boil, then reduce to a simmer. In a mixing bowl combine fish, eggs, salt, pepper, remaining 1/2 teaspoon (2 ml) sugar, grated carrots and onions, and matzo meal. Beat until thoroughly mixed. It should be shiny and fairly smooth. Moisten hands with water and shape table-spoonfuls (15 ml) of the mixture into balls the size of an egg. Place each fish ball in the broth. Cover and simmer for 1-1/2 hours. Chill thoroughly in the broth. Serve with grated horse-radish sauce.
Makes 8 servings

COULIBIAC

Very popular in Russia and Middle European countries, *coulibiac,* a hot salmon pâté, is a beautiful dish for a holiday buffet. Assemble in advance and bake later, if you like.

6 tablespoons (90 ml) fresh lemon
 juice
1/4 cup (50 ml) minced fresh dill
 weed, or
  1-1/2 tablespoons (22 ml) crushed
   dried dill weed
One 3-pound (1.5 kg) salmon fillet,
 skinned
Rich Brioche Dough, page 109
3 egg yolks
1 cup (250 ml) sour cream
2 cups (500 ml) cooked long-grain rice
Salt and white pepper to taste
1 pound (500 g) mushrooms, sliced
2 tablespoons (30 ml) butter
4 hard-cooked eggs, quartered
1 egg, beaten with
1 tablespoon (15 ml) milk

Mix together lemon juice and half of the dill weed. Place salmon in a ceramic or glass dish, pour lemon-dill mixture over, and cover and refrigerate 24 hours. Prepare Rich Brioche Dough and chill. Beat egg yolks until blended and mix in remaining dill and the sour cream. Add rice and season with salt and pepper. Sauté mushrooms in butter for 1 minute. Roll out half of the Rich Brioche Dough and trim into the shape of a whole salmon the size of the salmon fillet, plus a 1-inch (3 cm) border. Dry salmon with paper towels. Lay three-fourths of the rice mixture on the dough and place the salmon on top. Arrange hard-cooked eggs in 2 rows along the fish. Sprinkle remaining rice mixture between eggs and make a wide row of mushrooms down the middle. Roll out remaining dough for the top the same size as the bottom. Brush egg-milk mixture around the border of the bottom piece of dough. Place second piece of dough on top and crimp edges together to seal. Make a hole, 1 inch (3 cm) in diameter for a vent, placing it to simulate an eye. Use scraps of dough to make fins, and cut snips in the top piece of dough with scissors to simulate fish scales. Chill 10 minutes. Brush with remaining egg-milk mixture and bake in a preheated 350°F (180°C) oven for 1 hour or until golden brown. Cut in slices to serve.
Makes 10 to 12 servings

SALMON AND
SCALLOP QUENELLES

Petits brioches were rising, scarlet raspberry sherbet was churning, a stuffed *ballottine* of lamb was oven-braising, and Chef Michel Haudebert was poaching *quenelles* and sharing the nuances of his famous lobster sauce. He explained that although *quenelles,* or fish dumplings, are usually made with pike in France, salmon and scallops may be used as substitutes. The feather-light *quenelles* are glorious, but it is the lobster sauce that steals the show.

Quenelles
4 ounces (125 g) skinned salmon fillet
    or skinned and boned salmon steak
6 ounces (175 g) scallops
2 teaspoons (10 ml) salt
1/2 teaspoon (2 ml) white pepper
Pinch freshly grated nutmeg
2 egg whites
1/4 pound (125 g) unsalted butter, at
    room temperature
2 cups (500 ml) heavy cream
3 quarts (3 L) water

Lobster Sauce
1 pound (500 g) live lobster, cleaned
    and split in half lengthwise and
    coral and tomalley reserved (see
    page 16), or
    3 rock lobster tails (about 5 ounces
    or 150 g each), split in half
    lengthwise

3 tablespoons (45 ml) butter
1 tablespoon (15 ml) chopped onion
1-1/2 teaspoons (7 ml) chopped
    carrot
1 tablespoon (15 ml) chopped
    shallots or green onions (white
    part only)
1 large garlic clove, minced
6 tablespoons (90 ml) cognac
1 cup (250 ml) dry white wine or
    vermouth
2 tablespoons (30 ml) tomato paste
Salt and white pepper to taste
8 cups (2 L) Fish Stock, page 115
1 tablespoon (15 ml) chopped fresh
    tarragon, or
    1 teaspoon (5 ml) crushed dried
    tarragon
1 bay leaf
1-1/2 teaspoons (7 ml) chopped fresh
    thyme, or
    1/2 teaspoon (2 ml) crushed dried
    thyme
3 parsley sprigs
3 tablespoons (45 ml) unsalted butter
    at room temperature
3 tablespoons (45 ml) flour
Salt and white pepper to taste
1/2 cup (125 ml) heavy cream

To make *quenelles,* grind salmon and scallops in a food grinder, then transfer to a mixing bowl, add the salt, pepper, nutmeg, and egg whites and beat with an electric mixer for 5 to 7 minutes. Or grind fish in a food processor fitted with a steel blade, then add salt, pepper, nutmeg, and egg whites and process for about 2 minutes, or until mixture clings together in a firm mass. If you have used a food processor, transfer the fish mixture to a mixing bowl. Add butter to the fish mixture and beat with an electric mixer 2 to 3 minutes or until well blended. Very gradually pour in the cream and beat at medium high speed until mixture is light in texture. The mixture will turn a pale coral color and increase in volume as the cream is beaten in. Cover bowl and chill 1 to 1-1/2 hours.

To shape *quenelles,* select 2 spoons with a tapered egg shape about 2-1/2 inches (6 cm) long. Lightly butter a large platter and place beside the bowl of chilled fish paste. Fill a bowl with hot water and place alongside. Dip one spoon in hot water and scoop up a spoonful of fish paste. Dip the second spoon in hot water and invert over the spoonful of paste to shape it into a smooth oval, then to slide the oval off of the first spoon onto the buttered platter. Repeat, making about 18 *quenelles* in all. In a large soup kettle, heat water until warm. Slip 6 to 8 quenelles into the water, so that they do not touch, and bring just to the simmering point. Remove from heat and let stand 5 minutes. The *quenelles* should be firm but slightly puffed. Transfer to a warmed platter or plates and keep warm. Repeat with remaining *quenelles*.

To make sauce, in a large frying pan sauté the lobster, still in its shell, in melted butter with onion, carrot, shallots and garlic. Cook just until lobster shell turns red and the lobster meat becomes opaque. Pour in 3 tablespoons (45 ml) of the cognac, heat slightly, then light with a match and allow the cognac to flame until the flame dies. Add wine, tomato paste, and salt and pepper. Add Fish Stock, tarragon, bay leaf, thyme, and parsley. Simmer for 20 minutes. Remove lobster from pan, remove meat from the shell and slice; set aside. Cook the pan juices until slightly reduced. Mix 2 tablespoons (30 ml) of the butter with the reserved lobster coral and tomalley, if available. Blend in flour and add to sauce; cook and stir until thickened. Press through a sieve, discarding vegetables and herbs. Season with salt and pepper. Add remaining butter and the cream and remaining cognac. Heat gently; do not allow to boil. Serve the *quenelles* with Lobster Sauce spooned over and garnish with sliced lobster.
Makes 6 servings

ASPARAGUS AND CRAYFISH RAMEKINS

The Swedish pairing of crayfish and first-of-the-season asparagus makes a stunning entrée. Lobster or shrimp can substitute for crayfish.

1-1/2 pounds (750 g) asparagus spears, trimmed to 4- to 5-inch (10 to 13 cm) lengths
4 tablespoons (60 ml) butter
12 ounces (375 g) shelled cooked crayfish or medium shrimp, or diced cooked lobster meat
2 tablespoons (30 ml) cognac or Pernod
1/2 cup (125 ml) sour cream
2 ounces (50 g) Jarlsberg or Gruyère cheese, shredded (about 1/2 cup or 125 ml)
Salt, white pepper, and fresh or dried dill weed to taste
2 hard-cooked egg yolks, sieved
2 tablespoons (30 ml) chopped chives or parsley

Peel asparagus stems from tip to base with a small knife. Cook asparagus in a steamer or in boiling salted water for 5 to 7 minutes or until crisp-tender; drain and divide between 4 heated ramekins. Melt 2 tablespoons (30 ml) of the butter in a frying pan until it sizzles and barely starts to brown and pour it over asparagus. Melt remaining butter and sauté crayfish 1 minute. Pour in cognac, ignite, and shake pan until flame dies out. Spoon over asparagus. Heat sour cream and cheese in the pan drippings, stirring, until cheese melts. Season with salt, pepper, and dill and spoon over crayfish. Garnish with egg yolks and chives.
Makes 4 servings

TOASTED CRAB AND GRUYÈRE ON FRENCH ROLLS

This hot sandwich is a superstar and an old-time favorite of my family.

6 French sourdough rolls, split in half
3 tablespoons (45 ml) butter
1 pound (500 g) flaked cooked crab meat
6 ounces (175 g) Gruyère or Jarlsberg cheese, shredded (about 1-1/2 cups or 375 ml)
1/4 cup (50 ml) mayonnaise
2 tablespoons (30 ml) sour cream
1/3 cup (75 ml) pimiento-stuffed olives, sliced
2 green onions, chopped

Spread rolls with butter and toast lightly. Mix together crab, cheese, mayonnaise, sour cream, olives, and onions. Spread on top of one half of each roll. Place in a preheated 400°F (210°C) oven until heated through and lightly browned. Serve with other half of roll alongside.
Makes 6 servings

LOBSTER TAILS THERMIDOR

Lobster tails make gorgeous individual servings to finish off Thermidor style for a gala entrée. Assemble them in advance for last-minute reheating.

8 cups (2 L) water
1 onion, studded with 2 whole cloves
1 bay leaf
Few celery leaves
4 rock lobster tails (about 8 ounces or 250 g each)
1/4 pound (125 g) butter
3 tablespoons (45 ml) each dry sherry and dry white wine or vermouth
4 medium mushrooms, sliced
1/4 cup (50 ml) flour
1 cup (250 ml) hot milk
1/2 teaspoon (2 ml) salt
Dash white pepper and freshly grated nutmeg
Grated Parmesan cheese

In a large soup kettle bring water to a boil with onion, bay leaf, and celery leaves. Add lobster tails, bring to a boil again, skim off foam, and simmer 6 to 8 minutes or until tender. Remove from heat, drain, and cool. With a small pair of scissors, cut along both sides of the white underside of the shell and pull it off. Remove meat from the shell and cut meat into bite-sized pieces. Pat shells dry with paper towels. Melt 4 tablespoons (60 ml) of the butter in a large frying pan and dip shells in the butter to coat both sides. Remove shells, fan out tail fins, and arrange in a shallow baking pan. Melt 1 tablespoon (15 ml) of the butter in the same pan and sauté lobster meat 1 minute, stirring. Pour in wine and let cook down slightly; set aside. Sauté mushrooms 1 minute in 1 tablespoon (15 ml) of the butter; set aside. Melt remaining 2 tablespoons (30 ml) of the butter and blend in flour; cook 2 minutes, stirring; do not let flour brown. Stir in milk, salt, pepper, and nutmeg and cook and stir until thickened. Add lobster and pan juices and mix lightly. Spoon into shells. Sprinkle with cheese and arrange mushroom slices on top. Bake in a preheated 350°F (180°C) oven for 10 minutes or until heated through.
Makes 4 servings

LOBSTER FROMAGE WITH RUM

This last-minute seafood dish is superb for a late supper. As a substitute for rum try Pernod or aquavit with their spicy overtones.

2 tablespoons (30 ml) butter
8 ounces (250 g) cooked flaked lobster meat or crab meat
3 tablespoons (45 ml) light rum
1/2 cup (125 ml) heavy cream
3 tablespoons (45 ml) unsalted pistachios or toasted slivered blanched almonds
4 ounces (100 g) Jarlsberg or Gruyère cheese, shredded (about 1 cup or 250 ml)
2 English muffins, split, buttered, and toasted, or
2 puff pastry shells*, baked
2 tablespoons (30 ml) chopped parsley

Melt butter in a frying pan and sauté lobster 1 minute. Add rum and stir to coat. Add cream, nuts, and cheese and heat just until cheese melts and sauce is blended. Spoon over hot toasted muffins and sprinkle with parsley.
Makes 2 servings

*Purchase already baked from a bakery or buy frozen shells and bake at home.

HANGTOWN FRY

Hangtown Fry is a legendary dish invented during Gold Rush days to satisfy a wealthy miner who desired the most expensive foods in camp. Serve this oyster omelet with French-fried potatoes.

18 small to medium oysters, shucked
Salt and freshly ground black pepper
Fine cracker meal
8 eggs
Butter
1/4 cup (50 ml) milk
Crisp-fried bacon

Season oysters with salt and pepper and dip in cracker meal. Beat 2 of the eggs and dip oysters in beaten egg and then again in cracker meal. Heat a large frying pan, add enough butter to lightly coat the bottom and fry oysters in butter until golden brown on one side. Turn over. Beat remaining eggs until blended, beat in milk, and season with salt and pepper. Pour over oysters and cook slowly until eggs are set and lightly browned. During cooking, lift the cooked eggs with a spatula to let the uncooked part run underneath. To serve, fold in half and turn out on a heated platter. Garnish with bacon and serve immediately.
Makes 6 servings

SHELLFISH ON ICE

For a summer buffet serve shellfish nestled in an ice bed accompanied with several complementary sauces. It is amazingly simple to set forth. Blend the sauces a day or two in advance. Vary the shellfish selection according to the bounty of the fish market. Include raw clams or oysters on the half shell, if you like.

4 King crab legs (about 2 pounds or
    1 kg)
2 Dungeness crabs, cooked, cleaned
    and cracked (about 3 pounds or
    1.5 kg)
1 or 2 spiny lobsters, cooked and
    cracked, or
    6 rock lobster tails, cooked and
    split (about 2 pounds or 1 kg)
1 pound (500 g) jumbo shrimp,
    cooked, shelled, and deveined
Sauce Remoulade, page 122
Green Mayonnaise, page 119
Spicy Tomato Sauce, following

Arrange shellfish on a bed of crushed ice on a large serving platter or several platters. Set out the sauces in bowls alongside. Let guests help themselves.
Makes 12 servings

SPICY TOMATO SAUCE Mix together 1 cup (250 ml) chili sauce, 1 teaspoon (5 ml) Worcestershire sauce, several drops Tabasco sauce, dash ground allspice, and 1/3 cup (75 ml) fresh lemon juice. Cover and chill thoroughly. Makes about 1-1/3 cups (325 ml).

SEAFOOD TOSTADAS

For a gala Mexican late supper let guests assemble their own tostada.

4 corn tortillas
Corn or safflower oil
1 can (16 ounces or 450 g) refried
    beans, heated
1 small head iceberg lettuce, shredded
2 tomatoes, seeded and chopped
4 ounces (125 g) Monterey Jack or
    Cheddar cheese, shredded (about
    1 cup or 250 ml)
8 ounces (250 g) flaked cooked crab
    meat or lobster meat, or small
    cooked shrimp
1/2 recipe Guacamole, page 116
3 green onions, chopped
Pitted black olives

Fry tortillas until crisp and puffy in 1/2-inch (1 cm) hot oil. Drain on paper towels. Place tortillas on heated dinner plates and spoon refried beans over. Serve with bowls of lettuce, tomatoes, cheese, shrimp, Guacamole, green onions, and olives.
Makes 4 servings

Pasta & Rice Dishes

CREAMED FINNAN HADDIE

The English consider creamed smoked haddock a breakfast dish. It makes an unusual entrée for a late supper, as well.

1-1/2 pounds (750 g) finnan haddie
    (smoked haddock)
1-1/2 cups (375 ml) milk
3 tablespoons (45 ml) butter
8 ounces (250 g) mushrooms, sliced
3 tablespoons (45 ml) flour
1-1/4 cups (300 ml) hot chicken broth
1/3 cup (75 ml) heavy cream
1 teaspoon (5 ml) Dijon-style
    mustard
Dash Tabasco sauce
2 green onions, chopped
3 hard-cooked eggs, sliced
Salt and freshly ground black pepper
    to taste
Hot cooked long-grain rice
3 tablespoons (45 ml) chopped red
    bell pepper or sliced pimiento-
    stuffed olives

Place fish in a frying pan and pour milk over. Cover and simmer about 20 minutes or until flesh of fish separates when tested with a fork. Drain off and discard milk. Let fish cool, then break into bite-sized pieces, discarding bones. In a saucepan melt 1 tablespoon (15 ml) of the butter and sauté mushrooms for 1 minute; remove from pan with a slotted spoon and set aside. Melt remaining butter and blend in flour; cook and stir 2 minutes, not allowing flour to brown. Gradually stir in chicken broth, cooking and stirring until thickened. Stir in cream, mustard, Tabasco, mushrooms, onions, eggs, and fish. Season with salt and pepper and heat through. Serve over hot rice, garnished with pepper.
Makes 4 to 6 servings

RISOTTO AL SALMONE

A glorious specialty of the Villa d'Este hotel on the shore of Lake Como.

8 ounces (250 g) smoked salmon,
    diced or shredded
1/4 pound (125 g) butter
1/3 cup (75 ml) whiskey
1/2 cup (125 ml) heavy cream
6 cups (1.5 L) light chicken broth
1 small onion, minced
2 cups (500 ml) long-grain rice
Freshly ground black pepper
2 tablespoons (30 ml) grated
    Parmesan cheese

Sauté salmon in 2 tablespoons (30 ml) of the butter. Pour whiskey over and cook until liquid is almost evaporated. Add cream and cook 1 minute; set aside. In a large saucepan bring broth to a boil. Meanwhile, in another pan melt 2 tablespoons (30 ml) of the butter and sauté onion until it is translucent. Add rice and stir for about 3 minutes until every grain is opaque and butter-coated. Slowly add half of the boiling broth and cook, over low heat, uncovered, stirring occasionally until liquid is almost absorbed. Then slowly add remaining broth. Cook uncovered for 10 minutes, stirring occasionally. Add the salmon sauce. It will take about 20 minutes total cooking time for the rice to absorb the stock. Remove from heat and stir in pepper and remaining butter and the cheese. Cover pan and let stand 3 to 4 minutes before serving.
Makes 8 servings

SALMON KEDGEREE

Kedgeree is served for breakfast in England; it is a traditional part of the meal preceding a fox hunt. This dish is a fine way to utilize leftover baked salmon.

6 ounces (170 g) packaged mixed
    white and wild rice
2 tablespoons (30 ml) each butter and
    flour
1 teaspoon (5 ml) curry powder
1 cup (250 ml) Fish Stock, page 115,
    or clam juice
3 tablespoons (45 ml) dry sherry
1 pound (500 g) cooked or smoked
    salmon or cod, or
    16 ounces (450 g) canned salmon,
    drained
3 hard-cooked eggs
2 green onions, minced
Mango chutney

Cook rice in boiling salted water as directed on the package, but omit any enclosed seasonings. Meanwhile, melt butter and blend in flour and curry powder; cook 2 minutes, stirring. Gradually stir in Fish Stock and, stirring, cook until thickened. Stir in sherry. Flake salmon (if using canned, remove any bones) and add to rice. Pour sauce over, mix lightly, and turn into a buttered casserole. Separate the yolks from the whites of the eggs and sieve each separately (or use a grater to shred them finely). Arrange in alternating stripes across the top along with a central stripe of green onion. Pass chutney to spoon over.
Makes 6 servings

SEAFOOD RISOTTO

Mussels or clams are steamed and the broth is used to cook the rice for a seafood risotto.

3-1/2 pounds (1.75 kg) mussels or
    small hard-shelled clams
1 cup (250 ml) water
1/2 cup (125 ml) dry white wine or
    vermouth
1 medium onion, minced
1 garlic clove, minced
3 tablespoons (45 ml) butter
1 cup (250 ml) long-grain rice
3 tomatoes, peeled, seeded, and diced
1/2 cup (125 ml) water
8 ounces (250 g) cooked small shrimp
1/2 cup (125 ml) heavy cream
2 tablespoons (30 ml) minced parsley
3 tablespoons (45 ml) grated Parmesan
    cheese

Soak mussels in salted water for 30 minutes (see page 16), then scrub well under cold running water with a stiff-bristled brush. Cut off beards. Place in a large kettle with water and wine, cover, and steam 5 to 10 minutes, or until shells open; discard any mussels that do not open. Measure and reserve 1-1/2 cups (375 ml) of the broth. With a small knife remove mussels from shells and set aside. In a large frying pan cook onion and garlic in butter until soft, stirring occasionally. Add rice and stir over medium heat until rice is opaque, about 3 minutes. Add tomatoes and 1 cup (250 ml) of the reserved broth. Cover and simmer until liquid is absorbed, about 10 minutes. Add remaining broth and water and simmer until liquid is absorbed, about 10 minutes longer. Stir in mussels, shrimp, and cream; cover and cook 2 minutes longer. Spoon into a heated serving dish and sprinkle with parsley and cheese.
Makes 4 to 6 servings

SEAFOOD PAELLA

The colors in this dish present a striking palette: saffron rice, coral seafood, green asparagus and peas, and scarlet pimiento. One of my culinary discoveries on a sojourn in Spain was seafood-and-vegetable paella, without the usual chicken and sausage.

1 medium onion, minced
2 garlic cloves, minced
1 large tomato, peeled, seeded, and
    chopped
1/4 cup (50 ml) olive oil
1-1/2 cups (375 ml) long-grain rice
1/2 teaspoon (2 ml) saffron
1 cup (250 ml) Fish Stock, page 115,
    or clam juice
1-1/2 cups (375 ml) hot water
1/2 cup (125 ml) dry white wine or
    vermouth
12 jumbo shrimp in the shell
12 small hard-shelled clams
1 cooked, cleaned, and cracked
    crab, or
    6 cooked small rock lobster tails
1-1/2 pounds (750 g) peas, shelled and
    parboiled, or
    1 package (10 ounces or 280 g)
    frozen baby peas, blanched for 2
    minutes in boiling water
8 ounces (250 g) asparagus spears,
    parboiled
1 jar (2 ounces or 56 g) sliced
    pimiento
Lemon wedges

In a large frying pan or a 4-quart (4 L) flameproof casserole sauté onion, garlic, and tomato in oil until vegetables are glazed. Add rice, saffron, Fish Stock, water, and wine; bring to a boil, cover, and simmer 20 minutes or until liquid is absorbed. Arrange shrimp and clams on top, cover, and steam until clam shells open. Transfer to a large paella pan or serving casserole. Add the crab, peas, asparagus, and pimiento. Heat in a preheated 350°F (180°C) oven until heated through, about 15 minutes. Garnish with lemon wedges.
Makes 6 to 8 servings

SEAFOOD DIJON

A matchless seafood casserole that is excellent with hot rice and steamed fresh asparagus. For dessert consider fresh pineapple boats or a lemon tart studded with raspberries.

4 tablespoons (60 ml) butter
8 ounces (250 g) mushrooms, sliced
3 tablespoons (45 ml) flour
1-1/2 teaspoons (7 ml) Dijon-style
    mustard
3/4 cup (175 ml) Fish Stock,
    page 115, or chicken broth
1/2 cup (125 ml) half-and-half
1/4 cup (50 ml) dry white wine or
    vermouth
4 ounces (125 g) Jarlsberg or Gruyère
    cheese, shredded (about 1 cup or
    250 ml)
1 pound (500 g) cooked small shrimp
8 ounces (250 g) flaked cooked crab
    meat or lobster meat
3 tablespoons (45 ml) chopped parsley
Hot cooked long-grain rice

Melt 2 tablespoons (30 ml) of the butter in a frying pan, add mushrooms, and sauté 1 minute or just until glazed. Turn out of pan. Melt remaining butter and blend in flour; cook, stirring, for 2 minutes; do not let flour brown. Stir in mustard, Fish Stock, half-and-half, and wine and cook until thickened, stirring occasionally. Add cheese and heat until melted. Mix in mushrooms, shrimp, and crab meat and turn into a buttered baking dish. Bake in a preheated 375°F (190°C) oven 15 minutes or until heated through. Sprinkle with parsley and spoon over rice.
Makes 6 to 8 servings

SHRIMP JAMBALAYA

This classic American Creole dish is colorful, and quick to prepare.

1 small green bell pepper, chopped
1 small onion, chopped
2 garlic cloves, minced
2 tablespoons (30 ml) butter
4 ounces (125 g) mushrooms, sliced
1 teaspoon (5 ml) salt
1/4 teaspoon (1 ml) white pepper
2 medium tomatoes, peeled, seeded, and chopped, or
   1 can (8 ounces or 225 g) tomatoes
1-1/2 teaspoons (7 ml) cornstarch blended with
1 tablespoon (15 ml) water
1 pound (500 g) shrimp, shelled and deveined
1/4 cup (50 ml) dry sherry
Hot cooked long-grain rice

In a large frying pan sauté pepper, onion, and garlic in 1 tablespoon (15 ml) of the butter until glazed but not brown. Add mushrooms and remaining butter and sauté 1 minute. Season with salt and pepper and stir in tomatoes. Bring to a boil and stir in cornstarch and water; cook and stir until thickened. Add shrimp and simmer 3 to 5 minutes or until pink; add sherry and heat through. Serve over hot rice.

Makes 4 servings

SHRIMP PILAFF

It is hard to surpass the Greek way of finishing off a pilaff with sizzling-hot browned butter.

2 cups (500 ml) Fish Stock, page 115, or clam juice
1 pound (500 g) large shrimp in the shell
1 large onion, minced
2 stalks celery, minced
3 tablespoons (45 ml) olive oil
1 cup (250 ml) long-grain rice
2 medium tomatoes, peeled, seeded, and chopped
Salt and freshly ground black pepper to taste
4 tablespoons (60 ml) butter
3 tablespoons (45 ml) minced parsley

Bring the Fish Stock to a boil, add shrimp, and simmer 5 to 8 minutes or until shrimp turn pink. Remove with a slotted spoon and let cool, then shell and devein. Reserve broth. In an 8-cup (2 L) flameproof serving casserole, sauté onion and celery in oil until soft. Add rice and stir and cook until opaque and coated with oil. Measure out 2 cups (500 ml) reserved broth and add to rice along with tomatoes. Bring to a boil and simmer, covered, 20 to 25 minutes or until rice is tender. Arrange shrimp on top to heat through the last few minutes. Heat butter until sizzling and lightly browned and pour over shrimp and rice, fluffing lightly with a fork. Sprinkle with parsley and serve immediately.

Makes 4 servings

SHRIMP AND WILD RICE CASSEROLE

A show-stopper party casserole to make in advance.

2 cups (500 ml) wild rice
5 tablespoons (75 ml) butter
3 shallots or green onions (white part only), chopped
1 pound (500 g) small mushrooms, sliced
1 tablespoon (15 ml) fresh lemon juice
3 tablespoons (45 ml) flour
1-1/4 cups (300 ml) hot chicken broth
1/3 cup (75 ml) dry white wine or vermouth
1/2 teaspoon (2 ml) salt
1-1/2 teaspoons (7 ml) chopped fresh tarragon, or
    1/2 teaspoon (2 ml) crushed dried tarragon
1 teaspoon (5 ml) grated lemon peel
4 ounces (125 g) Gruyère or Jarlsberg cheese, shredded (about 1 cup or 250 ml)
1-1/2 pounds (750 g) medium shrimp, cooked, shelled, and deveined
2 tablespoons (30 ml) minced parsley

Turn rice into a strainer and wash thoroughly under cold running water. Let soak in water to cover for 1 hour; drain. Cook, covered, in simmering salted water to cover for 25 minutes or until almost tender; drain. Melt 2 tablespoons (30 ml) of the butter in a large frying pan, add shallots and sauté until soft. Add mushrooms to pan. Sprinkle with lemon juice and sauté 1 minute; set aside. In another pan melt remaining 3 tablespoons (45 ml) butter and blend in flour. Cook, stirring, 2 minutes; do not let flour brown. Pour in chicken stock and the wine and cook, stirring constantly, until thickened. Season with salt, tarragon, and lemon peel. Mix in half of the cheese. Combine sauce with wild rice, mushrooms, and shrimp, reserving a few shrimp for garnish. Spoon into a buttered 2-1/2-quart (2.5 L) casserole. Arrange reserved shrimp on top and sprinkle with cheese. Cover and bake in a preheated 350°F (180°C) oven for 20 minutes, or until heated through. Sprinkle with parsley.
Makes 8 servings

VERMICELLI WITH CLAM SAUCE

Without fresh steamed clams, canned ones stand in nicely. If tomatoes aren't at their peak of flavor it is better to substitute canned.

3 to 4 pounds (1.5 to 2 kg) butter, littleneck, or other small hard-shelled clams, or
    8 Pismo clams, or
    2 cans (7 ounces or 196 g each) minced clams
1/2 cup (125 ml) dry white wine or vermouth or water
2 garlic cloves, minced
2 shallots or green onions (white part only), chopped
3 tablespoons (45 ml) olive oil
4 medium tomatoes, peeled, seeded, and chopped, or
    1 can (16 ounces or 450 g) plum tomatoes, drained and chopped
1 can (6 ounces or 170 g) tomato paste
1 tablespoon (15 ml) minced fresh oregano or basil, or
    1 teaspoon (5 ml) crushed dried oregano or basil
1/4 cup (50 ml) dry white wine or vermouth
Salt and white pepper to taste

1 pound (500 g) fresh or dried vermi-
celli, tagliarini, or other thin pasta
1/3 cup (75 ml) minced parsley
2 ounces (50 g) Romano cheese,
grated (about 1/2 cup or 125 ml)

Soak clams in salted water for 30 minutes (see page 16). Scrub clams well
under cold running water with a stiff-
bristled brush. Place in a large kettle
with wine, cover pan, and steam 5 to
10 minutes, or until shells open; discard any clams that do not open. Remove clams from shells and mince. If
using canned clams, drain, and reserve
1/2 cup (125 ml) liquid. In a large
frying pan sauté garlic and shallots in
oil until soft. Add tomatoes, tomato
paste, oregano, wine, salt, and pepper;
cover and simmer 30 minutes. Add
clams and reserved clam broth and
simmer 5 minutes longer. Meanwhile,
cook pasta in a large amount of boiling
salted water until *al dente,* about 3 to
4 minutes for fresh pasta and 9 to 12
minutes for dried; drain well. Turn out
onto a large heated platter. Pour clam
sauce over and sprinkle with parsley
and cheese. If desired, pass additional
cheese.
Makes 4 to 6 servings

FILLET OF SOLE WITH NOODLES

This unusual combination of fish and
pasta is a specialty of Alsace, but is
popular throughout the French prov-
inces.

1-1/4 pounds (625 g) sole, orange
roughy, or turbot fillets
Salt and white pepper
1/2 cup (125 ml) dry white wine or
vermouth
1-1/2 tablespoons (25 ml) fresh lemon
juice
2 parsley sprigs
8 ounces (250 g) fresh fettuccine or
dried egg noodles
6 tablespoons (90 ml) butter
4 tablespoons (60 ml) flour
2 cups (500 ml) hot milk
Dash freshly grated nutmeg
3 tablespoons (45 ml) shredded
Gruyère or Jarlsberg cheese
3 tablespoons (45 ml) grated
Parmesan cheese
Butter

Cut fish into serving-sized pieces and
arrange in a heavy frying pan. Season
lightly with salt and pepper. Add wine,
lemon juice, and parsley. Cover and
simmer gently for 10 minutes, or until
flesh of fish separates when tested
with a fork. Discard parsley. Remove
fish to a platter and keep warm; reserve pan juices. Meanwhile, cook
noodles in boiling salted water until *al
dente*, about 3 or 4 minutes for fresh
pasta, 10 to 12 minutes for dried.
Drain well. Toss with 1 tablespoon
(15 ml) of the butter and keep warm.

Melt 4 tablespoons (60 ml) of the
butter in a saucepan. Blend in flour
and cook and stir 2 minutes; do not let
flour brown. Add milk all at once and
whisk until smooth, simmering over
low heat until thickened. Season with
nutmeg. Whisk reserved pan juices into
the sauce along with 2 tablespoons
(30 ml) of each cheese. Stir over low
heat until thick and smooth. Mix half
of the sauce into the noodles. Spoon
into a buttered shallow baking dish
and top with fish. Pour remaining
sauce over and sprinkle with remaining
cheese. Dot with butter and place under a broiler until sauce is bubbly and
light golden brown on top, about 5 to
7 minutes.
Makes 4 servings

PASTA WITH CRAB

Seafood and vegetables turn pasta into a meal in one dish.

8 ounces (250 g) zucchini, thinly sliced
2 tablespoons (30 ml) butter
3 medium mushrooms, thinly sliced
1 green onion, chopped
6 to 8 ounces (175 to 250 g) flaked cooked crab meat
1/2 cup (125 ml) chicken broth
2 teaspoons (10 ml) fresh lemon juice
1/4 teaspoon (1 ml) salt
Dash white pepper
1/2 teaspoon (2 ml) chopped fresh oregano, or
   1/8 teaspoon (.5 ml) crushed dried oregano
2 tablespoons (30 ml) heavy cream
1 ounce (25 g) Parmesan cheese, grated (about 1/4 cup or 50 ml)
4 ounces (125 g) fresh tagliarini or fettuccine, or dried spaghetti
Cherry tomatoes
Parsley sprigs

In a large frying pan sauté zucchini in butter until crisp-tender. Add mushrooms and onion and sauté a few seconds. Add crab meat, broth, lemon juice, salt, pepper, and oregano and simmer 1 minute. Stir in cream and 2 tablespoons (30 ml) of the cheese. Keep warm. Meanwhile, cook pasta in boiling salted water, allowing 3 to 4 minutes for fresh pasta and 10 to 12 minutes for dried, or until *al dente*; drain. Pour out on a heated platter, spoon crab sauce over and toss lightly. Sprinkle remaining cheese over and garnish with tomatoes and parsley.
Makes 2 to 3 servings

THAI-STYLE NOODLES WITH SEAFOOD

In Thailand, river raft vendors peddle exotic foods such as this noodle dish with pork and seafood.

12 ounces (375 g) dried fine egg or wheat noodles
1-1/4 cups (300 ml) safflower oil
4 ounces (125 g) lean pork, cut in matchsticks
4 ounces (125 g) shrimp, shelled and deveined
4 ounces (125 g) cooked crab meat
1 tablespoon (15 ml) each soy sauce and white vinegar
2 teaspoons (10 ml) anchovy paste
2 teaspoons (10 ml) sugar
1 teaspoon (5 ml) salt
Dash chili oil or pinch ground dried red chili pepper
4 eggs, slightly beaten
1 cup (250 ml) bean sprouts
2 green onions, chopped
Chopped fresh coriander

Drop noodles into boiling salted water. Cook 1 minute and drain well. Spread out on paper towels to dry. Heat 1 cup (250 ml) of the oil in a wok or a frying pan and fry noodles until crisp; remove and drain on paper towels. Heat remaining oil in wok or frying pan and sauté pork 2 to 3 minutes, or until no longer pink. Add shrimp, crab meat, soy sauce, vinegar, anchovy paste, sugar, salt, and chili oil and cook over low heat 2 to 3 minutes. Stir in eggs, sprouts, and green onions and cook and stir until just set. Stir in noodles. Turn out onto a platter and sprinkle with fresh coriander.
Makes 4 servings

Crêpes & Quiches

SALMON AND MUSHROOM CRÊPES

These rich salmon-filled crêpes can be assembled ahead for party serving.

Crêpes, following
1/4 cup (50 ml) chopped green onion
8 ounces (250 g) mushrooms, chopped
1/4 pound (125 g) butter
5 tablespoons (75 ml) flour
2 cups (500 ml) hot milk
1 cup (250 ml) heavy cream
3/4 teaspoon (3 ml) salt
Dash cayenne pepper
1 pound (500 g) cooked salmon, or
    16 ounces (450 g) canned salmon,
    drained
6 ounces (175 g) Jarlsberg or Gruyère
    cheese, shredded (about 1-1/2 cups
    or 375 ml)
1 ounce (25 g) Parmesan cheese,
    grated (about 1/4 cup or 50 ml)

Prepare Crêpes; stack and cover. Sauté onion and mushrooms in 2 tablespoons (30 ml) of the butter for about 1 minute; set aside. Melt remaining butter and blend in flour; cook 2 minutes, not allowing flour to brown. Stir in milk and cream. Cook, stirring, until thick and smooth. Season with salt and pepper. Flake salmon (if using canned, pick out any bones). Combine mushrooms, salmon, and about 3/4 cup (175 ml) of the sauce. Spoon a ribbon of salmon mixture down the center of each crêpe and roll up. Add Jarlsberg cheese to remaining sauce and heat until cheese melts. Spoon a thin layer of cheese sauce in the bottom of a buttered baking dish or individual ramekins. Arrange filled crêpes over sauce. Spoon remaining sauce over crêpes and sprinkle with Parmesan cheese. Bake in a preheated 375°F (190°C) oven for 30 minutes or until golden brown and bubbly.
Makes 6 servings

CRÊPES Place in a blender or beat with a wire whisk 2 eggs, 3/4 cup (175 ml) milk, 1/2 cup plus 1 tablespoon (140 ml) all-purpose flour, and 1/8 (.5 ml) teaspoon salt; blend until smooth. Let batter stand at least 30 minutes. Heat a 6-inch (15 cm) crêpe pan or skillet over medium heat, add 1/2 teaspoon (2 ml) butter, and tilt pan to coat surface. Pour in just enough batter to coat pan (about 2 tablespoons or 30 ml of batter) and tilt pan to cover entire surface. Cook until golden brown on the edges and dry on top, less than 1 minute. Turn out onto a plate. Repeat with remaining batter, adding butter as needed. Makes 12 crêpes.

CRAB AND MUSHROOM CRÊPE TART

This rates three stars! It is a beautiful party dish to assemble in advance for last-minute baking.

Crêpes, following
Mornay Sauce, following
8 ounces (250 g) flaked cooked crab
    meat or cooked small shrimp
8 ounces (250 g) mushrooms
2 green onions, chopped
1 tablespoon (15 ml) butter
8 ounces (250 g) cream cheese, at
    room temperature
1 egg
Salt and white pepper to taste
3 tablespoons (45 ml) grated Parmesan cheese
2 tablespoons (30 ml) chopped parsley

Prepare Crêpes; stack and cover. Prepare Mornay Sauce. Measure out 3/4 cup (175 ml) of the Mornay Sauce, cover, and set aside. Mix crab meat into remaining sauce and set aside. Sauté mushrooms and onions in butter. Beat cream cheese until creamy and beat in egg; mix in mushrooms and onions and season with salt and pepper. In a buttered baking dish place 1 crêpe and spread with one-fourth of the crab filling. Top with another crêpe and one-third of the mushroom filling; repeat. Cover the top crêpe with reserved Mornay Sauce and sprinkle with Parmesan cheese. Bake in a preheated 350°F (180°C) oven 15 to

20 minutes, or until heated through. Sprinkle with parsley and cut in wedges to serve.
Makes 8 servings

CRÊPES Place in a blender or beat with a wire whisk 4 eggs, 1-1/3 cups (325 ml) milk, 1 cup (250 ml) all-purpose flour, and 1/4 teaspoon (1 ml) salt; blend until smooth. Let batter stand at least 30 minutes. Heat a 9- to 10-inch (23 to 25 cm) crêpe pan or skillet over medium heat, add 3/4 teaspoon (4 ml) butter, and tilt pan to coat surface. Pour in just enough batter to coat pan (3 to 4 tablespoons or 45 to 60 ml) and tilt pan to cover entire surface. Cook until golden brown on the edges and dry on top, less than 1 minute. Turn out onto a plate. Repeat with remaining batter, adding butter as needed. Makes 8 crêpes.

MORNAY SAUCE In a saucepan melt 3 tablespoons (45 ml) butter and stir in 4 tablespoons (60 ml) flour. Cook and stir 2 minutes, not allowing flour to brown. Add 1/3 cup (75 ml) heavy cream to 1-1/2 cups (375 ml) hot Fish Stock, page 115, clam juice, or chicken broth. Mix into butter-flour mixture and cook until thickened, stirring occasionally. Add 1/4 teaspoon (1 ml) each salt and white pepper. Remove from heat and stir in 3 ounces (75 g) Gruyère cheese, shredded (about 3/4 cup or 175 ml).

SEAFOOD AND WATER CHESTNUT CRÊPES

Crêpes filled with fish or shellfish and water chestnuts, then covered with a topping that puffs up when broiled.

Crêpes, page 66
8 ounces (250 g) peas, shelled
2 tablespoons (30 ml) minced onion
5 tablespoons (75 ml) butter
1/3 cup (75 ml) flour
1/2 teaspoon (2 ml) salt
Dash white pepper
1 teaspoon (5 ml) chopped fresh tarragon, or
    1/4 teaspoon (2 ml) crushed dried tarragon
1-1/2 cups (375 ml) hot milk
1/2 cup (125 ml) dry white wine or vermouth
1 ounce (25 g) Parmesan cheese, grated (about 1/4 cup or 50 ml)
1 ounce (25 g) Gruyère cheese, shredded (about 1/4 cup or 50 ml)

1 pound (500 g) flaked cooked fish such as salmon, halibut, or turbot, or
8 ounces (250 g) each cooked small shrimp and flaked cooked crab meat
5 ounces (125 g) canned water chestnuts, drained and sliced
1/4 cup (50 ml) heavy cream, whipped

Prepare Crêpes, stack, and cover with a cloth. Cook peas in boiling salted water until just tender; set aside. In a large saucepan, sauté onion in butter until soft. Add flour and cook 2 minutes; do not brown. Add salt, pepper, and tarragon and gradually stir in milk and wine. Cook, stirring, until thickened. Set aside half of sauce for topping. To the remaining sauce, mix in half of the combined cheeses and the fish, water chestnuts, and peas. To assemble, place about 1/4 cup (50 ml) filling in a ribbon down the center of each crêpe, roll and lay seam side down in a buttered 9- by 13-inch (23 x 33 cm) baking pan. Fold the whipped cream into the reserved sauce, spoon over the crêpes, and sprinkle with remaining cheese. Bake in a preheated 375°F (190°C) oven for 20 minutes or until topping is golden brown.
Makes 6 servings

SALMON AND OLIVE QUICHE

Quiches are quick and simple to make using press-in pastry.

Press-In Pastry, following
4 eggs
1-1/4 cups (300 ml) half-and-half
3 tablespoons (45 ml) chopped parsley
1 shallot or green onion (white part only), chopped
Salt and freshly ground black pepper
1 pound (500 g) cooked salmon, or 16 ounces (450 g) canned salmon, drained
3 ounces (75 g) Cheddar or Swiss cheese, shredded (about 3/4 cup or 175 ml)
1/2 cup (125 ml) sliced pitted black or pimiento-stuffed olives
2 teaspoons (10 ml) butter

Prepare pastry; chill. Beat eggs until blended and mix in half-and-half, parsley, shallots, salt, and pepper. Flake salmon (if using canned, remove any bones) and place in the pastry shell with cheese and olives. Pour custard over. Dot with butter. Bake in a preheated 425°F (220°C) oven for 10 minutes; reduce heat to 375°F (190°C) and bake 20 minutes longer or until set. Remove from pan and cut into wedges to serve.
Makes 8 servings

PRESS-IN PASTRY Place in a mixing bowl 1-1/4 cups (300 ml) all-purpose flour, 1/4 pound (125 g) butter, and 1/2 teaspoon (2 ml) salt. Cut butter into flour with a pastry cutter until crumbly. Add 2 egg yolks or 1 whole egg and mix until blended. Press into bottom and sides of an 11-inch (28 cm) fluted flan pan with a removable bottom or a 10-inch (25 cm) pie pan. Chill 20 minutes before using.

CRAB QUICHE

A rich quiche with a hint of sherry.

Press-In Pastry, page 68
6 ounces (175 g) Gruyère or Jarlsberg cheese, shredded (about 1-1/2 cups or 375 ml)
2 shallots or green onions (white part only), finely chopped
2 tablespoons (30 ml) butter
8 ounces (250 g) flaked cooked crab meat
2 tablespoons (30 ml) dry sherry
1/4 teaspoon (1 ml) freshly grated nutmeg
5 eggs
1-1/2 cups (375 ml) half-and-half or milk
1/2 teaspoon (2 ml) salt
Freshly ground black pepper

Prepare Press-In Pastry and chill. Sprinkle shell with half the cheese. Sauté shallots in 1 tablespoon (15 ml) of the butter until soft. Add crab meat and sauté 1 minute. Add sherry and nutmeg and cook until liquid almost disappears. Beat eggs just until blended and stir in half-and-half, salt, and pepper. Mix in crab meat mixture and remaining cheese. Spoon into cheese-lined shell. Dot with remaining butter. Bake in a preheated 425°F (220°C) oven for 10 minutes; reduce heat to 375°F (190°C) and continue baking 20 to 25 minutes or until custard is set and golden brown. Remove from pan and cut into wedges to serve.
Makes 8 servings

SEAFOOD QUICHE

A sprinkling of nutmeg scents this mixed seafood pie.

Press-In Pastry, page 68
2 shallots or green onions (white part only), chopped
2 tablespoons (30 ml) butter
6 ounces (175 g) cooked small shrimp
5 eggs
1-1/4 cups (300 ml) half-and-half or milk
1 can (7 ounces or 196 g) minced clams with juice
1/2 teaspoon (2 ml) salt
1/4 teaspoon (1 ml) freshly grated nutmeg
6 ounces (175 g) Gruyère or Swiss cheese, shredded (about 1-1/2 cups or 375 ml)

Prepare pastry and chill. Sauté shallots in 1 tablespoon (15 ml) of the butter until soft. Add shrimp and sauté 1 minute. Beat eggs until blended and mix in half-and-half, clams, salt, nutmeg, cheese, and shrimp. Turn into pastry-lined pie pan and dot with remaining butter. Bake in a preheated 425°F (220°C) oven for 10 minutes; reduce heat to 375°F (190°C) and bake 20 minutes longer or until set and golden brown. Remove from pan and cut into wedges to serve.
Makes 8 servings

TOMATO AND SHRIMP QUICHE

Flour tortillas form a wafer-thin crust for this Mexican-inspired quiche. Serve hot as an appetizer or first course or cold for a picnic dish.

2 tablespoons (30 ml) butter
Two 12-inch (30 cm) flour tortillas
4 ounces (125 g) Monterey Jack or Cheddar cheese, shredded (about 1 cup or 250 ml)
4 green onions, chopped
2 firm ripe tomatoes
Flour
Salt and freshly ground black pepper
3 tablespoons (45 ml) diced canned peeled green chilies
4 ounces (125 g) cooked small shrimp
4 eggs
1 cup (250 ml) milk
Salt and freshly ground black pepper

Melt butter in a 9-inch (23 cm) pie pan. Dip tortillas in melted butter to coat both sides and place in pan, overlapping the tortillas to cover the bottom and sides of the pan. Sprinkle with half of the cheese and half of the onions. Slice tomatoes 1/4-inch (6mm) thick and dip in flour. Place in pie pan in a single layer. Sprinkle with salt and pepper. Scatter the remaining onions, chilies, and shrimp over the tomatoes. Beat eggs until blended; stir in milk and season with salt and pepper and pour over. Sprinkle with remaining cheese. Bake in a preheated 400°F (210°C) oven for 25 minutes or until custard is barely set in the center. Cut into wedges to serve.
Makes 8 to 10 appetizer or first-course servings or 6 entrée servings

Mousses & Soufflés

CLAM SOUFFLÉ

Freshly dug clams, steamed and chopped, are delicious in this soufflé, though canned ones may be substituted. It makes a showy luncheon or supper entrée or an exciting first course.

3 pounds (1.5 kg) small hard-shelled clams, or
2 cans (7 ounces or 196 g each) minced clams, drained
1/2 cup (125 ml) dry white wine or vermouth or water
2 tablespoons (30 ml) butter
3 tablespoons (45 ml) flour
3/4 cup (175 ml) milk
1/2 teaspoon (2 ml) salt
White pepper to taste
1/8 teaspoon (.5 ml) freshly grated nutmeg
4 ounces (125 g) Swiss or Gruyère cheese, shredded (about 1 cup or 250 ml)
4 eggs, separated

Soak clams in salted water 30 minutes (see page 16). Scrub well under cold running water with a stiff-bristled brush. Place in a large kettle with water or wine, cover, and steam 5 to 10 minutes, or until shells open; discard any clams that do not open. Remove clams from shells and mince. In a saucepan, melt butter, blend in flour and cook 2 minutes. Gradually stir in milk and, stirring constantly, cook until thickened. Season with salt, pepper, and nutmeg. Mix in cheese, egg yolks, and clams. Beat egg whites until stiff, glossy peaks are formed, and fold in. Turn into a buttered 6-cup (1.5 L) soufflé dish and bake in a preheated 375°F (190°C) oven for 30 minutes, or until golden brown, puffed, and set. Serve at once.
Makes 6 servings

SHRIMP AND TURBOT SOUFFLÉ

Puréed fish and Jarlsberg cheese flavor this shrimp-studded soufflé. If it is necessary to reheat this dish, it will achieve a surprising puff the second time.

12 ounces (375 g) turbot, cod, whiting, or sole fillets
1-1/2 cups (375 ml) milk
4 tablespoons (60 ml) butter
4 ounces (125 g) cooked small shrimp
2 tablespoons (30 ml) dry sherry
1/4 cup (50 ml) flour
3/4 teaspoon (4 ml) each salt and dry mustard
Dash Tabasco sauce
6 eggs, separated
4 ounces (125 g) Jarlsberg or Gruyère cheese, shredded (about 1 cup or 250 ml)
2 egg whites
3 tablespoons (45 ml) grated Parmesan cheese

In a blender or a food processor fitted with a steel blade, purée fish with 1/3 cup (75 ml) of the milk. In a frying pan melt 1 tablespoon (15 ml) of the butter, add shrimp, and sauté 1 minute. Add sherry and simmer 1 minute. Remove shrimp from pan with a slotted spoon and set aside, reserving pan juices. Melt remaining butter and blend in flour, salt, and mustard; cook 2 minutes, stirring constantly. Add remaining milk and reserved pan juices and cook until thickened, stirring. Add fish purée and cook 1 minute. Stir in Tabasco sauce, egg yolks, and Jarlsberg cheese. Beat the 8 egg whites until stiff, glossy peaks are formed and fold in. Spoon into a buttered 10-inch (25 cm) round casserole or 10-cup (2.5 L) soufflé dish with a foil collar. (To make a foil collar, take a sheet of aluminum foil 4 inches (10 cm) longer than the circumference of the dish, and fold it in half lengthwise. Butter the upper half and place around outside of dish, making a double fold to keep in place.) Scatter the shrimp and Parmesan cheese on top. Bake in a preheated 375°F (190°C) oven for 30 minutes or until puffed, golden brown, and set through.
Makes 6 to 8 servings

SALMON AND SOLE MOUSSE RING

Sometimes called a fish turban, this eye-catching pale-pink hot fish mousse is striped with white fish fillets. It is a cooking class favorite, as it's a honey of an entrée for entertaining.

1 pound (500 g) sole, orange roughy, or turbot fillets
1 pound (500 g) salmon fillets, skinned
5 egg yolks
1 cup (250 ml) light cream
1 teaspoon (5 ml) salt
1-1/2 teaspoons (7 ml) chopped fresh tarragon, or
   1/2 teaspoon (2 ml) crushed dried tarragon
1 cup (250 ml) heavy cream
Watercress sprigs
Hollandaise Sauce, page 124, or
   Mousseline Sauce, page 125

Cut the sole into strips about 2 inches (5 cm) wide and 6 inches (15 cm) long. Lightly butter a 6-cup (1.5 L) ring mold. Lay fish strips, light side down, in the mold at even intervals like the spokes of a wheel, letting them lap over the sides if necessary. Set aside. In a blender or a food processor fitted with a steel blade purée salmon with egg yolks and enough of the light cream to make a smooth purée. Turn into a bowl and stir in remaining light cream, salt, and tarragon. Whip heavy cream until stiff and fold in. Spoon the mousse into the ring mold on top of the fish fillets, spreading evenly. Tuck any overlapping fillets down into the mousse. Place mold in a pan containing 1 inch (3 cm) hot water and bake in a preheated 350°F (180°C) oven for 35 minutes, or until set. Remove from oven and let cool on a rack 10 minutes. Slip a knife around the edge, then turn upside down onto a heated platter to unmold. Garnish with watercress sprigs and pass Hollandaise or Mousseline Sauce.
Makes 8 servings

SALMON MOUSSE

This pretty, cold salmon mold is ideal for a luncheon or a first course and is a fine way to use leftover baked salmon.

2 envelopes (2 tablespoons or 30 ml) unflavored gelatin
2/3 cup (150 ml) clam juice
1 pound (500 g) cooked salmon, or
   16 ounces (450 g) canned salmon, drained (remove any bones)
1 tablespoon (15 ml) anchovy paste
1 teaspoon (5 ml) green peppercorns, or
   1 tablespoon (15 ml) capers
1 shallot or green onion (white part only), chopped
1/4 cup (50 ml) fresh lemon juice
1-1/2 teaspoons (7 ml) chopped fresh tarragon, or
   1/2 teaspoon (2 ml) crushed dried tarragon
Several drops Tabasco sauce
2 cups (500 ml) heavy cream
Watercress sprigs
Sour-Cream Shallot Sauce, page 116

Sprinkle gelatin over clam juice in a saucepan and let stand until softened. Heat over low heat just until dissolved and let cool to room temperature. In a blender or a food processor fitted with a steel blade, purée the salmon, anchovy paste, green peppercorns, shallot, lemon juice, tarragon, Tabasco, and gelatin mixture. Whip cream until stiff and fold in. Pour into a lightly oiled 6-cup (1.5 L) loaf pan or fish mold and chill until set, about 8 hours. Dip pan or mold in a pan of hot water and unmold mousse onto a platter. Garnish with watercress sprigs. Pass Sour Cream Shallot Sauce to spoon over.

Makes 8 first-course servings or 4 entrée servings

HALIBUT AND SHRIMP MOUSSE

A pink and green ribbon of shrimp and herbs stripes the center of this snow-white fish mousse. Present it hot or cold for a luxurious first course or entrée.

1 pound (500 g) halibut fillets
3 egg whites
1 cup (250 ml) heavy cream
3/4 teaspoon (4 ml) salt
1/4 teaspoon (1 ml) each white pepper and freshly grated nutmeg
1-1/2 teaspoons (7 ml) chopped fresh dill weed, or
    1/2 teaspoon (2 ml) crushed dried dill weed
2 tablespoons (30 ml) each minced parsley and chives
6 ounces (175 g) cooked small shrimp
Hollandaise Sauce, page 124, Buerre Blanc, page 124, or Green Mayonnaise, page 119

In a blender or a food processor fitted with a steel blade, purée fish until smooth. Add egg whites and blend until smooth. Add cream and blend until cream is absorbed. Add salt, pepper, nutmeg, and dill weed and blend in quickly. Butter a 9- by 5-inch (23 by 13 cm) loaf pan and spread bottom with half of the fish mousse. Cover with the herbs and then the shrimp. Spread remaining fish mousse over all. Cover pan with buttered waxed paper and place in a pan containing 1 inch (3 cm) of hot water. Bake in a preheated 350°F (180°C) oven for 35 to 40 minutes, or until firm. Let cool 10 minutes, then unmold. Serve hot with Hollandaise Sauce or Beurre Blanc or cold with Green Mayonnaise.

Makes 6 to 8 servings

SCALLOP MOUSSE WITH TOMATO CREAM SAUCE

For a gorgeous party dish, blanket a smooth mousse with a creamy tomato sauce.

2 pounds (1 kg) scallops
2 shallots or green onions (white part only), chopped
2 tablespoons (30 ml) butter
Salt and white pepper
1/2 cup (125 ml) dry white wine or vermouth
3 egg yolks
2 cups (500 ml) heavy cream
Salt, white pepper, and freshly grated nutmeg to taste
Chopped parsley or chives
Tomato Cream Sauce, following

Measure out 1 cup (250 ml) of the scallops; if using sea scallops cut each into 3 or 4 pieces. In a large frying pan sauté shallots in butter until glazed. Add scallops and season with salt and pepper; sauté 1 minute. Add wine and simmer 1 minute. Remove sautéed scallops from pan with a slotted spoon; reserve juices. Using a blender or food processor fitted with a steel blade, add half of the remaining uncooked scallops and 1 of the egg yolks to the container and blend until smooth. Add 1 cup (250 ml) of the cream and purée about 1 minute. Remove from container and add the second batch of scallops and repeat with the 2 remaining egg yolks. Season with salt, pepper, and nutmeg. Add remaining cream and purée. Combine the two mixtures and the sautéed scallops. Heavily butter an 8-cup (2 L) mold and spoon in the mousse mixture. Place a buttered sheet of aluminum foil on top of the mold, cutting it to fit. Set mold in a pan containing 1 inch (3 cm) hot water and bake in a preheated 375°F (190°C) oven for 40 to 45 minutes, or until set. Remove aluminum foil and unmold mousse onto a heated platter. Garnish with parsley. Serve with Tomato Cream Sauce.
Makes 8 to 10 servings

TOMATO CREAM SAUCE Melt 2 tablespoons (30 ml) butter in a saucepan and sauté 1 small chopped onion until glazed. Add 3 large peeled, seeded, and diced tomatoes and salt and freshly ground black pepper to taste. Cook over high heat until most of the juices evaporate. Boil the reserved scallop juices from the recipe for Scallop Mousse until reduced to about 1/4 cup (50 ml). Add to tomato mixture along with 1 cup (250 ml) heavy cream and 1-1/2 teaspoons (7 ml) minced fresh basil or 1/2 teaspoon (2 ml) crushed dried basil. Simmer until reduced to a thick consistency. Makes about 2-1/2 cups (625 ml).

SCALLOP MOUSSE VARIATION Use 1 pound (500 g) each skinned salmon fillet and scallops in place of the 2 pounds (1 kg) scallops.

SOLE MOUSSELINE WITH NANTUA SAUCE

This cloud-light mousseline makes an elegant first course or entrée. It is similar to one served at Barrier, a two-star restaurant in Tours.

8 ounces (250 g) sole or halibut fillets
4 eggs
4 tablespoons (60 ml) butter, at room temperature
1/2 teaspoon (2 ml) salt
1/8 teaspoon (.5 ml) each white pepper and freshly grated nutmeg
1 cup (250 ml) heavy cream
2 teaspoons (10 ml) fresh lemon juice
Nantua Sauce, page 118

Place fish, eggs, butter, salt, pepper, and nutmeg in a blender or a food

processor fitted with a steel blade. Purée until smooth. Add cream and lemon juice and continue to blend until thick and lemon colored, about 5 minutes. Pour into 6 heavily buttered 6-ounce (175 ml) soufflé dishes, ramekins, or custard cups and place in a 9- by 13- by 2-inch (23 by 33 by 5 cm) pan. Pour hot water into the pan to within 1/2 inch (1 cm) of the top of the cups. Bake in a preheated 350°F (180°C) oven for 35 to 40 minutes, or until mousseline is puffy and lightly browned. Remove from hot water bath. Run a knife around the edges to release. Unmold onto heated plates and spoon Nanuta Sauce over.
Makes 6 servings

SOLE AND SHRIMP MOUSSE

Individual hot seafood mousses are perfect for a guest luncheon or a party first course.

12 ounces (375 g) sole or orange
    roughy fillets
4 ounces (125 g) cooked small shrimp
2 egg yolks
2 eggs, separated
3/4 cup (175 ml) half-and-half
3 tablespoons (45 ml) flour
1 teaspoon (5 ml) salt
1/8 teaspoon (.5 ml) freshly grated
    nutmeg
1 tablespoon (15 ml) each fresh
    lemon
    juice and brandy or cognac
1 cup (250 ml) heavy cream
Shrimp Sauce, following

In a blender or food processor fitted with a steel blade, purée fish fillets and shrimp and turn out into a bowl. Add the 4 egg yolks, one at a time, beating until smooth after each addition. Beat in half-and-half, flour, salt, nutmeg, lemon juice, and brandy. Whip cream until stiff and fold in. Beat egg whites until stiff, glossy peaks are formed and fold in. Turn into 6 buttered individual baking molds, about 1 cup (250 ml) each. Place in a pan containing 1 inch (3 cm) hot water and bake in a preheated 350°F (175°C) oven for 25 minutes or until puffed and set. Let cool 5 minutes, then unmold on heated serving plates. Serve with Shrimp Sauce.
Makes 6 servings

SHRIMP SAUCE Boil 2 cups (500 ml) Fish Stock, page 115, until reduced to 1 cup (250 ml). Beat 2 egg yolks until light; blend in 2 teaspoons (10 ml) cornstarch and 1/2 cup (125 ml) light cream. Pour in the hot Fish Stock and cook, stirring, until thickened. Stir in 1 tablespoon (15 ml) dry sherry and 1/2 cup (125 ml) cooked small shrimp or flaked cooked crab meat. Makes 2 cups (500 ml).

MUSTARD MOUSSE WITH LOBSTER

Two kinds of mustard season this creamy mousse, providing a spicy contrast to the lobster.

1 envelope (1 tablespoon or 15 ml)
    unflavored gelatin
2 tablespoons (30 ml) cold water
1/2 cup (125 ml) hot water
2 tablespoons (30 ml) sugar
4 teaspoons (20 ml) dry mustard
1-1/2 tablespoons (25 ml) Dijon-style
    mustard
1/2 cup (125 ml) white wine vinegar
2 eggs, lightly beaten
Salt and white pepper to taste
3/4 cup (175 ml) heavy cream
Watercress or lettuce leaves
1 pound (500 g) flaked cooked lobster
    meat or crab meat, or cooked small
    shrimp

Soften gelatin in cold water; add hot water and stir over heat until gelatin is completely dissolved. Let cool until syrupy. In the top of a double boiler mix together sugar, mustards, vinegar, eggs, salt, and pepper. Cook over simmering water, stirring, until mixture coats a spoon; let cool to room temperature. Whip cream until stiff and fold in. Turn into oiled individual molds such as small soufflé dishes or custard cups. Chill several hours until firm. Unmold on watercress and surround with lobster.
Makes 6 servings

Sautéed & Stir-Fried Fish

SAUTÉEING, STIR-FRYING, PAN-FRYING, AND DEEP-FRYING

The French word *sauter* means "to jump" and describes the technique of cooking food rapidly in an open pan, using a small amount of fat. Sautéeing is especially suited to small whole fish such as trout or smelt, or thin pieces of tender-fleshed fish that will cook through quickly. Because butter burns easily, it is best to use part butter and part oil for sautéeing, or you may use clarified butter. The surface of fish should be patted dry with paper towels or dusted lightly with cornstarch or flour. Add fish to the pan after the butter and oil have heated to the point of fragrance and the butter has ceased to foam. Do not crowd the fish; it needs ample room in the pan so that it will cook quickly and brown evenly. After the fish is cooked, transfer it to a heated platter and, if you like, add wine, lemon juice, or other liquid to the pan drippings, boil to reduce slightly, and pour over the fish; serve immediately.

Stir-frying is an Oriental version of sautéeing in which small pieces of food are cooked very rapidly in hot oil. A wok is ideal for stir-frying, as its design allows the food to be evenly covered with oil and to be easily stirred and quickly cooked, but a heavy frying pan may be substituted. The wok or frying pan should be heated over high heat until a drop of water sizzles when added to the pan. Oil is then added to the pan and heated almost to the smoking point. Peanut oil is traditional in Chinese cooking, but corn or safflower oil may be substituted. Food is added to the hot oil and cooked very briefly while being constantly stirred.

Sautéeing and stir-frying have been emphasized in the following recipes as opposed to pan-frying and deep-frying, because foods cooked by the first two methods are lower in calories. Pan-frying is defined as cooking food partially covered in hot fat. Pan-fried fish are usually coated with a batter. If you wish to pan-fry small whole fish or fillets, dip the fish first in a mixture of eggs beaten with a small amount of milk, then roll the fish in fresh bread crumbs, cornstarch or flour, cornmeal, wheat germ, or finely ground almonds or filberts. Add fat, preferably polyunsaturated oil, to a heavy frying pan to a depth of 1/4 to 3/8 inch (6 mm to 1 cm), and heat the oil to the point of fragrance. Add fish and cook, allowing about 5 minutes cooking time on each side for a piece of fish 1 inch (3 cm) thick.

To deep-fry fish, heat peanut, corn, cottonseed, safflower, or soybean oil to 375°F (190°C), adjusting heat a few degrees lower for small fish or small pieces of fish, and a few degrees higher for large fish or large chunks of fish. Fish may be dipped first in milk or beaten eggs, then in cornstarch or flour, or dried carefully with paper towels, then coated with a batter. Cook fish completely submerged in the hot oil. If necessary, cook in batches to avoid crowding, and make sure that the oil is returned to its original temperature each time a new batch of fish is added. Drain cooked fish well on paper towels.

MARINATED FISH THE GREEK WAY

On a visit to Athens, my Greek cousins presented me with a dinner featuring two fish courses: a charcoal-grilled *melanouri* fish, and this dish of fried fish fillets in an herb-vinegar sauce.

1 pound (500 g) red snapper, sole, or
   turbot fillets or halibut steaks
Salt and freshly ground black pepper
Cornstarch or flour
2 to 3 tablespoons (30 to 45 ml)
   olive oil
2 garlic cloves, minced
1 teaspoon (5 ml) minced fresh
   rosemary, or
   1/4 teaspoon (1 ml) crushed dried
   rosemary
3 tablespoons (45 ml) white wine
   vinegar

Season fish with salt and pepper and dust lightly with cornstarch. In a large frying pan sauté fish in the oil, turning to brown both sides, until flesh of fish separates when tested with a fork. Remove to a platter (if fish is to be served hot, use a heated platter and keep fish warm). Add garlic, rosemary, and vinegar to pan. Stirring, scrape up drippings and let cook down slightly. Spoon over fish and serve hot or chilled.
Makes 3 to 4 servings

MAHI-MAHI HAWAIIAN STYLE

Fresh papaya and avocado slices lend a refreshing, tropical flourish to butter-browned mahi-mahi. Mangos can be used in place of papaya when in season.

1 pound (500 g) mahi-mahi, pompano,
   sole, or turbot fillets
3 tablespoons (45 ml) fresh lemon or
   lime juice
Salt and white pepper
Cornstarch or flour
3 tablespoons (45 ml) butter
1 tablespoon (15 ml) safflower oil
1/4 cup (50 ml) chopped unsalted
   macadamia nuts or sliced almonds
1 small papaya, halved, seeded, peeled,
   and sliced
1 avocado, peeled and sliced
1 lime or lemon, cut in wedges

Season fish with 1 tablespoon (15 ml) of the lemon juice and salt and pepper. Dip in cornstarch to coat all sides and shake off excess. In a large frying pan sauté fish fillets in 1 tablespoon (15 ml) of the butter and the oil, turning to brown both sides, until flesh of fish separates when tested with a fork. Transfer to a heated platter. Add the remaining butter to the pan, add nuts, and sauté until golden brown. Add remaining lemon juice, stirring to scrape up nuts and drippings, and spoon over fish. Arrange papaya slices over fish and arrange avocado slices alongside. Garnish with lime wedges.
Makes 4 servings

MAHI-MAHI WITH SAUTÉED BANANAS

Hot orange-glazed banana slices smother lightly curried fish fillets, a dish reminiscent of Caribbean fare.

1 pound (500 g) mahi-mahi, swordfish, or other white-fleshed
   fish fillets
Salt and white pepper
Cornstarch or flour
2 tablespoons (30 ml) butter
1 tablespoon (15 ml) safflower oil
1 teaspoon (5 ml) curry powder
2 bananas, peeled and sliced on the
   diagonal
2 tablespoons (30 ml) orange juice
   concentrate
1 tablespoon (15 ml) chopped pistachio nuts (optional)
1 lime or lemon, cut in wedges

Season fish with salt and pepper and dust lightly with cornstarch. In a large frying pan sauté fish in 1 tablespoon (15 ml) of the butter and the oil until flesh of fish separates when tested with a fork. Transfer to a heated platter and keep warm. Melt remaining butter in pan, add curry and bananas; cook 1 minute. Turn over and add juice concentrate, and cook 1 minute longer. Spoon over the fish and sprinkle with nuts. Garnish with lime wedges.
Makes 4 servings

JAMAICAN PICKLED FISH

A colorful mixture of vegetables in a sprightly sauce permeates browned fish fillets. Serve this dish hot or cold.

1 large onion, thinly sliced
1 red and 1 green bell pepper, seeded and sliced lengthwise into strips
2 carrots, thinly sliced
4 tablespoons (60 ml) olive oil
1 cup (250 ml) water
1/4 cup (50 ml) white vinegar
Salt and freshly ground black pepper to taste
1-1/4 pounds (575 g) red snapper or other white-fleshed fish fillets
Salt and freshly ground black pepper

In a large frying pan sauté onion, peppers, and carrots in 2 tablespoons (30 ml) of the oil until soft but not browned. Add water, vinegar, salt, and pepper and simmer, covered, for 10 to 12 minutes, or until vegetables are tender. Meanwhile, heat remaining oil in another frying pan and sauté fish until browned on both sides and flesh of fish separates when tested with a fork. Season with salt and pepper and transfer to a heated platter. Pour vegetable sauce over fish.
Makes 4 servings

SALMON WITH SORREL

Frères Troisgros, the French three-star restaurant in Roanne, inspires this specialty. A peek into the kitchen reveals the staff filleting beautiful coral salmon for this dish.

1 cup (250 ml) Fish Stock, page 115, or clam juice
1 cup (250 ml) dry white wine or vermouth
2 shallots or green onions (white part only), chopped
2 teaspoons (10 ml) cornstarch blended with
2 teaspoons (10 ml) water
1 cup (250 ml) heavy cream
2 teaspoons (10 ml) fresh lemon juice, or to taste
Salt and freshly ground black pepper to taste
3 tablespoons (45 ml) unsalted butter
1-1/2 pounds (750 g) salmon fillets, skinned
1 cup (250 ml) finely shredded sorrel leaves

Combine Fish Stock, wine, and shallots in a saucepan and boil until reduced by one half. Stir in cornstarch paste and cook until slightly thickened. In a separate pan boil cream until reduced by one half. Combine the cream with the wine sauce and add lemon juice, salt, and pepper. Add 1 tablespoon (15 ml) of the butter and stir until butter is blended in. Keep warm.

Cut salmon into serving-size pieces and remove the dark brown part of the flesh. Lay each piece between 2 sheets of waxed paper and pound gently but firmly with the flat side of a cleaver until tripled in dimensions. In a large frying pan melt the remaining 2 tablespoons (30 ml) butter and sauté salmon about 30 seconds on each side. Spoon about 1/3 cup (75 ml) sauce onto each heated plate. Sprinkle each with about 3 tablespoons (45 ml) shredded sorrel. Top with salmon, place a small nest of sorrel on top of each serving and serve at once.
Makes 4 servings

SNAPPER WITH PEARS AND FILBERTS

One of the most delightful finishing touches for seafood is a specialty of Scandia Restaurant in Los Angeles. There fish fillets are garnished with julienne-cut winter pears, grapes, and toasted filberts, all sparked with lemon peel.

1 Winter Nellis pear, peeled and cut in julienne
2 tablespoons (30 ml) fresh lemon juice
1 pound (500 g) red snapper or other white-fleshed fish fillets
Salt and white pepper
Cornstarch or flour
3 tablespoons (45 ml) butter
1 tablespoon (15 ml) safflower oil
1/4 cup (50 ml) chopped filberts or slivered almonds
1 teaspoon (5 ml) grated lemon peel
1/2 cup (125 ml) seedless green grapes

Place pear in lemon juice to marinate while preparing fish. Season fish with salt and pepper and dust lightly with cornstarch. In a large frying pan sauté fish in 1 tablespoon (15 ml) of the butter and the oil until browned on both sides and flesh of fish separates when tested with a fork. Transfer to a heated platter. Add remaining butter to the pan and heat just until it starts to brown. Add nuts and toast lightly, stirring. Add lemon peel, grapes, and pears and barely heat through. Spoon over fish.
Makes 4 servings

STUFFED SEA BASS

A superb Oriental way of stuffing a whole fish.

One 1-1/2-pound (750 g) whole black sea bass or rockfish
2 sweet Chinese pork sausages
4 ounces (125 g) scallops
1/2 cup (125 ml) canned water chestnuts, drained
3 green onions, chopped
Salt
1/3 cup (75 ml) peanut oil or safflower oil
Fresh coriander sprigs

Prepare fish for stuffing (see page 15) and remove any residual bones. Pat dry with paper towels. In a meat grinder or a food processor fitted with a steel blade, grind the sausages, scallops, and water chestnuts separately until each is the size of small peas (or finely chop with a sharp knife). Then mix all 3 ingredients together with the green onions. Gently stuff the bass with this mixture. Tie fish closed at several points with cotton string. Sprinkle fish with salt and gently rub with 1 tablespoon (15 ml) of the oil. In a wok or large frying pan, heat remaining oil over medium heat and ease fish into pan, shaking pan occasionally to make certain that fish cooks evenly and does not stick. Let cook about 10 minutes on each side, turning it gently with 2 large spatulas. Transfer to a heated platter and garnish with fresh coriander.
Makes 4 to 5 servings

FISH GALLIANO

A contemporary Italian recipe uses fennel and Galliano to make a superb sauce for fish.

1-1/2 pounds (750 g) sole, turbot, orange roughy, or flounder fillets
Salt and freshly ground black pepper
Cornstarch or flour
1/3 cup (75 ml) slivered blanched almonds
3 tablespoons (45 ml) unsalted butter
1 tablespoon (15 ml) olive oil
1/4 cup (50 ml) each Galliano liqueur and fresh lemon juice
1 tablespoon (15 ml) chopped fresh fennel leaves, or
    1/2 teaspoon (2 ml) dried fennel seeds or crushed dried dill weed

Season fish with salt and pepper and dust lightly with cornstarch. In a large frying pan sauté almonds in 1 tablespoon (15 ml) of the butter until golden brown; remove from pan and set aside. Add remaining butter and the oil to pan and sauté fish, turning to brown both sides. Pour in Galliano and lemon juice and add fennel. Let the sauce simmer and cook the fish several minutes or until flesh of fish separates when tested with a fork, spooning juices over fish as it cooks. Sprinkle with nuts and serve at once.
Makes 4 to 6 servings

SHAD ROE WITH HERBS

Fresh herbs are delightful addition to delicate sautéed roe.

3 tablespoons (45 ml) butter
1 tablespoon (15 ml) safflower oil
2 pairs shad roe
Salt and freshly black ground pepper
1 tablespoon (15 ml) fresh lemon juice
3 tablespoons (45 ml) minced parsley
1 tablespoon (15 ml) minced chives
1 teaspoon (5 ml) chopped fresh tarragon, or
    1/4 teaspoon (1 ml) crushed dried tarragon

In a large frying pan sauté roe in 1 tablespoon (15 ml) of the butter and the oil, turning to cook both sides, about 10 to 12 minutes in all. Season with salt and pepper and transfer to a heated platter; keep warm. Melt remaining butter in the pan and stir in lemon juice, scraping up drippings. Add parsley, chives, and tarragon and spoon over roe.
Makes 2 to 3 servings

FISH WITH DIJON MUSTARD SAUCE

This is a fast and delectable French way to serve fish: bathed in a creamy wine-spiked mustard sauce.

1-1/2 pounds (750 g) sole or turbot fillets
Salt and white pepper
Cornstarch or flour
1 tablespoon (15 ml) each butter and olive oil
1/2 cup (125 ml) dry white wine or vermouth
Dash freshly grated nutmeg
1-1/2 tablespoons (25 ml) Dijon-style mustard
1/2 cup (125 ml) heavy cream
Chopped parsley

Cut fish into serving pieces and season with salt and pepper. Dust lightly with cornstarch. In a large frying pan sauté fish in butter and oil until brown on both sides, for a total of about 5 to 7 minutes, or until flesh of fish separates when tested with a fork. Transfer to a heated platter and keep warm. Pour wine into the pan and scrape up the drippings. Add nutmeg, mustard, and cream and bring to a boil, stirring, until sauce thickens slightly. Pour sauce over fish and sprinkle with parsley.
Makes 4 to 6 servings

NORWEGIAN SOLE AND SHRIMP

This colorful seafood entrée is dazzling to behold and to savor. I discovered it years ago in Bergen, Norway, at a little upstairs restaurant.

4 sole or turbot fillets (about 1-1/4 pounds or 625 g)
Salt and white pepper
Cornstarch or flour
3 tablespoons (45 ml) butter
1 tablespoon (15 ml) safflower oil
5 ounces (150 g) mushrooms, sliced
2 teaspoons (10 ml) fresh lemon juice
4 ounces (125 g) cooked small shrimp
3/4 cup (175 ml) cherry tomatoes, halved
2 tablespoons (30 ml) minced parsley
1 lemon, cut in wedges

Season fish with salt and pepper and dust lightly with cornstarch. In a large frying pan sauté fillets in 1-1/2 tablespoons (25 ml) of the butter and the oil until browned on both sides and flesh of fish separates when tested with a fork. Transfer to a heated platter and keep warm. Add remaining butter to pan, add mushrooms, sprinkle with lemon juice, and sauté until glazed. Add shrimp and tomatoes and heat through. Spoon over fish fillets, sprinkle with parsley, and garnish with lemon wedges.
Makes 4 servings

SOLE GRENOBLOISE

Try to find the wonderful big imported capers for this fast fish sauté. And consider such non-traditional fish as whiting or hake. I savored it made with *fera*, a European fish, at a terrace restaurant in Ouchy, Switzerland, beside Lake Leman.

1 lemon
4 sole, turbot, whiting, or hake fillets (about 1-1/4 pounds or 625 g)
Salt and white pepper
Cornstarch or flour
4 tablespoons (60 ml) butter
1 tablespoon (15 ml) safflower oil
2 tablespoons (30 ml) fresh lemon juice
2 tablespoons (30 ml) extra-large capers

Cut half of the lemon into thin rounds for garnish. With a vegetable peeler remove the yellow part of the peel from the remaining lemon half; cut peel into fine slivers and set aside. Season fish with salt and pepper and coat lightly with cornstarch. In a large frying pan sauté fish in 1 tablespoon (15 ml) of the butter and the oil until lightly browned on both sides and flesh of fish separates when tested with a fork. Remove to a heated platter and keep warm. Add remaining butter to pan drippings and heat slowly until butter turns light brown. Add lemon juice, capers, and lemon peel, and stir to blend. Spoon over fish and garnish with lemon slices.
Makes 4 servings

TROUT AMANDINE

Butter-toasted almonds sparked with lemon is a favorite Continental topping for fresh trout.

6 medium trout
Milk
Salt and white pepper
Cornstarch or flour
5 tablespoons (75 ml) butter
1 tablespoon (15 ml) safflower oil
1/2 cup (125 ml) sliced almonds
2 tablespoons (30 ml) fresh lemon juice
Lemon wedges dipped in minced parsley

Dip trout in milk, season with salt and pepper, then dust with cornstarch. In a large frying pan sauté trout in 2 tablespoons (30 ml) of the butter and the oil until golden brown on both sides and flesh of fish separates when tested with a fork. Transfer to a heated platter. Add remaining butter to pan, add almonds and heat, shaking pan, until nuts are golden brown. Add lemon juice and spoon over fish. Garnish with lemon wedges.
Makes 6 servings

CAPERED TURBOT WITH VEGETABLE TOPPING

This dish goes from pan to table in less than ten minutes. Hunt for extra-large capers from the Mediterranean to adorn it.

1-1/2 pounds (750 g) turbot, sole, or other white-fleshed fish fillets
Salt and white pepper
Cornstarch or flour
2 tablespoons (30 ml) butter
1 tablespoon (15 ml) safflower oil
8 ounces (250 g) mushrooms, sliced
4 green onions, chopped
1 tablespoon (15 ml) capers
3 tablespoons (45 ml) chopped parsley
1 tablespoon (15 ml) chopped chives or fresh basil
4 large tomatoes, peeled, seeded, and diced

Cut fish into serving pieces and season with salt and pepper. Dust lightly with cornstarch. In a large frying pan sauté fish in 1 tablespoon (15 ml) of the butter and the oil until brown on both sides and flesh of fish separates when tested with a fork. Transfer to a heated platter. Add remaining butter to pan; add onions and sauté 1 minute. Sprinkle with capers, parsley, chives, and tomatoes and heat 30 seconds. Spoon over fish.
Makes 6 servings

TURBOT WITH ORANGE SAUCE

A bright, tangy citrus sauce is an excellent topping for quickly sautéed fish fillets.

1-1/2 pounds (675 g) turbot, hake, or whiting fillets
Salt and white pepper to taste
Cornstarch or flour
2 tablespoons (30 ml) butter
1 tablespoon (15 ml) safflower oil
2 teaspoons (10 ml) grated orange peel
1 teaspoon (5 ml) grated lemon peel
1/2 cup (125 ml) fresh orange juice
3 tablespoons (45 ml) fresh lemon juice
2 teaspoons (10 ml) sugar
1 orange, thinly sliced
Watercress or parsley sprigs

Season fish fillets with salt and pepper and dust lightly with cornstarch. In a large frying pan sauté fish in 1 tablespoon (15 ml) of the butter and the oil until brown on both sides and flesh of fish separates when tested with a fork. Sprinkle with citrus peels and pour in orange and lemon juice. Cook over medium heat, allowing juices to bubble up around fish and cook until flesh of fish separates when tested with a fork. Transfer fish to a heated platter and spoon sauce over. Melt remaining butter and sugar in the pan, add orange slices, and cook over high heat until slightly caramelized, about 1 minute. Spoon alongside fish and garnish with watercress.
Makes 4 servings

ARNO AND RICK'S ABALONE

From two seafood experts came this recipe, which originally began, "First catch an abalone."

1 abalone
Salt and white pepper
Cornstarch or flour
1 egg
2 tablespoons (30 ml) milk
French bread crumbs
2 tablespoons (30 ml) each butter and safflower oil

Cut out the foot muscle of the abalone with a flexible-bladed knife. Slice off the bottom 1/2 inch (1 cm) of the foot and discard, as it is quite tough. Slice the remainder of the foot into 1/2-inch (1 cm) sections. Pound until the fibers begin to separate and the thickness is reduced to 1/4 inch (6 mm). Season with salt and pepper; dust with cornstarch. Beat egg and mix in milk. Dip the abalone in egg mixture and then in bread crumbs. In a large frying pan sauté in butter and oil for 40 seconds per side. Serve immediately.
Make 2 to 4 servings,
depending on size of abalone.

ABALONE WITH MUSHROOM SAUCE

A fresh mushroom sauce masks abalone steaks for a gloriously rich seafood entrée.

6 abalone steaks
2 egg yolks, lightly beaten
3/4 cup (175 ml) fine dry bread crumbs
1/4 cup (50 ml) olive oil
1 garlic clove, minced
Salt and white pepper
2 tablespoons (30 ml) butter
8 ounces (250 g) mushrooms, sliced
1 tablespoon (15 ml) fresh lemon juice
1 teaspoon (5 ml) grated lemon peel
1 cup (250 ml) half-and-half
1 tablespoon (15 ml) cornstarch blended with
1 tablespoon (15 ml) cold water
2 tablespoons (30 ml) dry white wine or vermouth
Salt and white pepper to taste
1 ounce (25 g) Romano cheese, grated (about 1/4 cup or 50 ml)

Pound abalone steaks until fibers begin to separate and thickness is reduced to 1/4 inch (6 mm). Dip abalone steaks in beaten egg yolks and then in bread crumbs, coating both sides. In a large frying pan, sauté abalone and garlic in the olive oil until abalone is golden brown on both sides. Season with salt and pepper and transfer to a buttered flameproof casserole. Add butter and mushrooms to frying pan, sprinkle with lemon juice and lemon peel, and sauté for 1 minute or just until glazed; spoon over abalone. Pour half-and-half into frying pan and bring to a boil. Stir in cornstarch paste and cook until thickened. Stir in wine and season with salt and pepper. Spoon sauce over abalone and mushrooms and sprinkle with cheese. Place under the broiler until lightly browned.
Makes 6 servings

CRAB IN CILANTRO BUTTER

Here is a hot variation of cracked crab that I discovered in a little Portuguese fish café years ago.

1/4 pound (125 g) unsalted butter
1/4 cup (50 ml) each fresh lemon juice and chopped fresh coriander
1 large Dungeness crab (about 3 pounds or 1.5 kg), cooked, cleaned, and cracked
Lemon wedges

Heat butter, lemon juice, and coriander in a large frying pan. Add crab pieces and cook until just heated through. Serve with lemon wedges.
Makes 2 servings

CURRIED CRAB AND SNOW PEAS

Snow peas and crab meat bound in a spicy sauce produce a festive Oriental dish.

8 ounces (250 g) cooked crab meat
1 teaspoon (5 ml) minced ginger root
2 teaspoons (10 ml) rice wine or dry sherry
1 tablespoon (15 ml) peanut oil or safflower oil
2 teaspoons (10 ml) curry powder
2 green onions, chopped
1/2 cup (125 ml) Fish Stock, page 115, or clam juice or chicken stock
1/4 teaspoon (1 ml) salt
1/2 cup (125 ml) sliced canned water chestnuts
12 ounces (375 g) snow peas, stems removed
1-1/2 teaspoons (7 ml) cornstarch blended with
1 tablespoon (15 ml) cold water

Mix crab meat with ginger root and wine and marinate for 30 minutes. Heat oil in a wok or large frying pan over medium heat. Add curry powder and green onions and stir-fry lightly. Add crab and stir-fry 1 minute. Pour in Fish Stock and add salt, water chestnuts, and pea pods and cook 2 minutes. Stir in the cornstarch paste and cook, stirring, until slightly thickened, about 1 minute.
Makes 2 to 3 servings

LOBSTER À L'AMERICAINE

A delectable, classic dish—best with Northern lobsters.

2 live lobsters (about 1-1/2 pounds or 750 g each)
1/3 cup (75 ml) each chopped onion, celery, and carrot
1 tablespoon (15 ml) chopped parsley
1 tablespoon (15 ml) each butter and olive oil
2 tablespoons (30 ml) brandy or cognac
2/3 cup (150 ml) dry white wine or vermouth
2/3 cup (150 ml) Fish Stock, page 115, or consommé
2 medium tomatoes, peeled, seeded, and diced
Salt and freshly ground black pepper to taste
1 tablespoon (15 ml) minced parsley

Split and clean lobsters (see page 16), reserving tomalley, or liver, and coral, or roe, if any. Remove legs and break in half. With a large knife, cut tail meat, shell and all, into 1-inch (3 cm) sections; crack claws. In a large frying pan, sauté onion, celery, carrot, and parsley in butter and oil until vegetables are soft. Add lobster pieces, legs, and claws; cook until shells turn red. Add brandy, light with a match, and cook until flame dies. Remove lobster from pan and keep warm. Add wine, stock, and tomatoes to pan; simmer 15 minutes. Discard herbs, add lobster, tomalley, and coral (if available); heat well. Add salt and pepper. Serve with parsley sprinkled on top and accompanied with picks to remove any stubborn lobster meat from the shells.
Makes 6 servings

LOBSTER AND EGG STIR-FRY

This swift stir-fry can be very versatile, depending on the choice of available seafood.

2 celery stalks
2 medium carrots
4 tablespoons (60 ml) peanut or safflower oil
4 green onions, chopped
1 cup (250 ml) bean sprouts
3 tablespoons (45 ml) chili sauce
1 tablespoon (15 ml) soy sauce
8 ounces (250 g) cooked flaked lobster meat or crab meat, or cooked shrimp, or raw scallops (if using sea scallops, cut in quarters)
4 eggs, slightly beaten
Salt

Slice celery and carrots on the diagonal into wafer-thin slices. Heat oil in a wok or large frying pan, add celery, carrots, and onions and stir-fry 2 to 3 minutes, or until tender-crisp. Add bean sprouts, chili sauce, soy sauce, and seafood and heat through. Season eggs with salt and pour into pan. Continue cooking, stirring, until eggs are set. Serve immediately.
Makes 4 servings

SCALLOPS WITH SHALLOT AND BASIL SAUCE

Scallops make a superlative entrée or first course to sauté at the last minute.

1 pound (500 g) scallops
1 tablespoon (15 ml) fresh lemon juice
1/4 teaspoon (1 ml) salt
Dash white pepper
1 tablespoon (15 ml) olive oil
2 tablespoons (30 ml) butter
3 shallots or green onions (white part only), minced
2 garlic cloves, minced
2 tablespoons (30 ml) dry white wine or vermouth
1-1/2 teaspoons (7 ml) chopped fresh basil, or
1/2 teaspoon (2 ml) crushed dried basil
1 tablespoon (15 ml) each chopped parsley and chives

If using sea scallops, cut them in quarters. Sprinkle scallops with lemon juice, salt, and pepper. In a large frying pan heat olive oil and 1 tablespoon (15 ml) of the butter until it sizzles and add shallots; sauté 1 minute. Add scallops and sauté on both sides, about 5 minutes. Add garlic, wine, basil, and remaining butter, and stir to blend sauce with drippings: Spoon into scallop shells and sprinkle with parsley and chives.
Makes 4 entrée servings or 6 first-course servings

SHRIMP SAUTÉ ITALIAN STYLE

In Italy this simple, elegant dish would be made with the native *scampi*; here it works just as well with jumbo shrimp.

1 garlic clove, minced
1 green onion (white part only) or shallot, chopped
1 tablespoon (15 ml) each butter and olive oil
8 ounces (250 g) jumbo shrimp, shelled and deveined
1/2 cup (125 ml) Fish Stock, page 115, or clam juice
1/4 cup (50 ml) dry white wine or vermouth
2 teaspoons (10 ml) cornstarch mixed with
1 tablespoon (15 ml) cold water
2 tablespoons (30 ml) minced parsley

In a large frying sauté garlic and onion in butter and oil until soft. Add shrimp and sauté until shrimp turn pink, about 2 minutes. Remove from pan and keep warm. Pour in Fish Stock and wine and bring to a boil. Stir in cornstarch paste and, stirring, cook until thickened. Spoon sauce into individual ramekins and arrange shrimp on top. Sprinkle with parsley.
Makes 2 servings

STIR-FRIED SHRIMP WITH GREEN ONIONS

Serve these sauce-coated shrimp either cold as an appetizer or hot as a main course. Cooking the shrimp in the shell intensifies their succulence. Shell just before serving, or let guests shell their own.

12 ounces (375 g) large shrimp in the shell
4 tablespoons (60 ml) peanut or safflower oil
1 bunch green onions, cut in 1-inch (3 cm) lengths
1/2 teaspoon (2 ml) salt
2 tablespoons (30 ml) each soy sauce and rice wine or dry sherry
1-1/2 teaspoons (7 ml) sugar

With a small pair of scissors, slit the shells on the backs of the shrimp, but do not remove them. Remove the veins. Rinse shrimp under cold running water and drain well on paper towels. Heat a wok or frying pan over high heat for a few seconds. Add 1 tablespoon (15 ml) of the oil, then add green onions and salt and stir-fry 30 seconds. Turn out of pan onto a platter. Add remaining oil to pan and heat. Add shrimp and stir-fry until shrimp turn pink, about 2 minutes. Add the soy sauce, wine, and sugar and stir-fry a few seconds. Return onions to pan and heat through.
Makes 3 entrée servings or about 30 appetizers

STIR-FRIED SQUID

Classic Oriental seasonings transform squid.

2 pounds (1 kg) small squid
2 tablespoons (30 ml) peanut or safflower oil
4 green onions, cut into 1-inch (3 cm) lengths
1/2 cup (125 ml) sliced canned bamboo shoots
2 slices ginger root, chopped
3 tablespoons (45 ml) each soy sauce and rice wine or dry sherry
1 tablespoon (15 ml) cornstarch blended with
3 tablespoons (45 ml) cold water

Clean squid (see page 17) and rinse well. Chop the tentacles finely and cut squid in half lengthwise, then in 1/2-inch (1 cm) crosswise pieces. Heat oil in a wok or large frying pan. Add squid and stir-fry 30 seconds. Add green onions, bamboo shoots, and ginger and stir-fry 1 minute. Add soy sauce and rice wine and stir-fry 2 minutes longer. Stir in cornstarch paste and cook, stirring, until sauce thickens and becomes translucent. Serve immediately.
Makes 4 to 6 servings

Grilled & Broiled Fish

GRILLING AND BROILING

Full-flavored, fatty fish such as salmon, albacore, mackerel, lake trout, and bluefish are ideal for grilling over charcoal because the smoky flavor of the coals does not overpower the flavor of the fish. Fish steaks, whole fish, and fish fillets are all good choices for grilling or broiling (whole fish can be split with the backbone left in, or the backbone may be removed as in Butterfly-Filleting, page 15). Brush fish well with oil or melted butter. A hinged grill is a great convenience when cooking over hot coals. When broiling fish in an oven it is helpful to line the broiling pan with buttered foil. The broiler should be preheated for 10 minutes before fish is cooked. Baste fish once or twice while cooking; use oil and/or melted butter, or a liquid such as wine, lemon juice, or a marinade. Steaks and whole fish should be turned once during the cooking process; fillets and split fish do not need turning. For a piece of fish 1 inch (3 cm) thick, allow 5 minutes cooking time on each side. Fillets, whole flat fish, fish steaks 1 inch (3 cm) thick or less, and split fish should be cooked 2 to 3 inches (5 to 8 cm) from heat; thick fish steaks or large fish should be cooked 4 to 5 inches (10 to 13 cm) from heat.

FISH KEBABS TERIYAKI

Firm-fleshed fish such as halibut, swordfish, mahi-mahi, or salmon are excellent to cut into chunks to grill for kebabs. The teriyaki marinade cooks to a golden-brown caramelized finish with a subtle sweetness. This recipe may be adapted to fish steaks.

One 2-pound (1 kg) piece halibut, swordfish, mahi-mahi, salmon, or other firm-fleshed fish
1/2 cup (125 ml) rice wine or dry sherry
1/4 cup (50 ml) soy sauce
1 tablespoon (15 ml) fresh lemon juice or white vinegar
1 garlic clove, minced
2 slices ginger root, slivered, or 1/4 teaspoon (1 ml) ground ginger
3 tablespoons (45 ml) peanut or safflower oil

Cut fish into 1- by 1-1/2-inch (3 by 4 cm) pieces, removing skin and bones. Place fish in a bowl. Combine rice wine, soy sauce, lemon juice, garlic, ginger root, and oil and pour over fish. Cover and chill for 2 hours, turning occasionally. Thread fish chunks on skewers and cook over low coals (or place under a broiler) for about 10 to 15 minutes or until flesh of fish separates when tested with a fork, basting occasionally with the remaining marinade.
Makes 6 servings

PACIFIC ISLANDS BROILED SNAPPER

Papaya slices are dipped in marinade and broiled for an accompaniment to broiled fish.

1-1/2 pounds (750 g) red snapper, sole, rockfish, ono, or turbot fillets
3 tablespoons (45 ml) soy sauce
2 tablespoons (30 ml) each rice wine or dry sherry, fresh lemon juice, and peanut or safflower oil
1 green onion, chopped
1 teaspoon (5 ml) chopped ginger root
1 papaya, peeled, halved, and seeded

Cut fish into serving pieces. Mix together the soy sauce, rice wine, lemon juice, oil, onion, and ginger in a shallow dish. Place fish in marinade and let stand 30 minutes, turning once. Remove fish from marinade and place on a broiling pan. Place under a broiler, turning once, until golden brown on both sides and flesh of fish separates when tested with a fork; place on a heated platter. Slice papaya and dip slices in marinade. Broil until just heated through. Arrange papaya slices around fish and serve immediately.
Makes 6 servings

GRILLED ALBACORE
WITH CUCUMBER SAUCE

Albacore is the most aristocratic member of the tuna family. The steaks are superb grilled and served with a cool cucumber sauce.

5 tablespoons (75 ml) butter
1 garlic clove, minced
1/4 cup (50 ml) fresh lemon juice
2 tablespoons (30 ml) chopped parsley
Salt and white pepper
2 pounds (1 kg) albacore steaks,
    skinned and cut into serving pieces
Cucumber Sauce, page 116

Melt butter and blend in garlic, lemon juice, and parsley. Season lightly with salt and pepper. Arrange fish steaks on a greased grill over hot coals or under a broiler. Baste often with lemon-butter and cook, turning once, until flesh of fish separates when tested with a fork, about 10 minutes. Remove to a platter and spoon Cucumber Sauce alongside.
Makes 6 servings

INDIAN-STYLE
PLANKED SALMON

The centuries-old American Indian way of barbecuing butterflied salmon is an extraordinary treat. The smoky, moist salmon is perfectly complemented with a chilled Chardonnay. A beach site is ideal for this dish. Originally the salmon was pinned to a split alder limb with cedar skewers. You will need the following: a board about 3 feet (90 cm) long and 1-1/2 feet (45 cm) wide, a 5-foot-long (1.5 m) wooden stake, heavy-duty aluminum foil, 2 nails, a spool of wire, a hammer or a rock to drive the nail, and a wire cutter.

One 6- to 8-pound (3 to 4 kg) whole
    salmon (or larger, if preferred)
Fresh lemon juice mixed with
Melted unsalted butter
Salt and white pepper

Remove head, tail, and fins of salmon. Split it down the middle so it lies flat, but do not cut all the way through the back of the fish. Cut bones away from meat and discard. At the barbecue site build a fire in front of a rock or hill that will reflect the heat. Cover one side of the plank with aluminum foil. Drive a nail part way into the top of one end of plank. Center salmon on plank skin side down. Cut 5 lengths of wire and secure fish onto plank at intervals along the length of the fish, twisting the ends of the wire together. Fasten end of stake to nail at top of plank with wire. Placing stake at an angle behind plank to prop it up, stand plank at about a 75° angle in front of the hot fire. Place a sheet of foil under bottom of plank and crimp edges upward to catch juices and keep sand off plank. Cook 40 to 50 minutes, or until flesh of fish separates when tested with a fork, basting occasionally with lemon juice and butter. Season with salt and pepper. To serve, lay plank flat and serve directly from it.
Makes 12 to 14 servings

SALMON STEAKS FLORENTINE

Spinach makes a festive backdrop for broiled salmon steaks.

2 large bunches spinach (about 1
   pound or 500 g each)
Salt, white pepper, and freshly grated
   nutmeg to taste
1/4 cup (50 ml) heavy cream
4 salmon steaks (1-1/2 to 2 pounds or
   750 g to 1 kg)
1/4 pound (125 g) unsalted butter,
   melted
3 tablespoons (45 ml) fresh lemon
   juice
1 teaspoon (5 ml) grated lemon peel
Salt and white pepper to taste

Wash spinach under cold running water; do not dry. Chop spinach and cook, covered, in a large frying pan just until wilted. Squeeze out excess moisture and season with salt, pepper, and nutmeg. Stir in cream, heat thoroughly, and turn into a buttered serving dish; keep warm. Arrange fish steaks on a broiler pan and drizzle with 2 tablespoons (30 ml) of the melted butter. Place under a broiler for about 7 to 8 minutes on each side, or until fish is lightly browned and flesh of fish separates when tested with a fork. Meanwhile, combine the remaining butter, lemon juice, and lemon peel and season with salt and white pepper. Arrange salmon steaks on top of spinach. Pour lemon-butter over fish.
Makes 4 servings

SALMON FILLETS FLAMBÉ

A Copenhagen discovery: grilled salmon fillets flamed at tableside with an aromatic anise liqueur.

Lemon Tarragon Butter, following
2 to 2-1/2 pounds (1 to 1.25 kg)
   salmon fillets, skinned
4 tablespoons (60 ml) butter
1/4 cup (50 ml) minced parsley
3 shallots or green onions (white part
   only), chopped
1-1/2 teaspoons (7 ml) chopped fresh
   tarragon, or
   1/2 teaspoon (2 ml) crushed dried
   tarragon
2 tablespoons (30 ml) Pernod or other
   anise-flavored liqueur

Prepare Lemon Tarragon Butter and brush fish with it. Place fish in a hinged wire broiler. Place skin side down on a grill over hot coals. Baste once or twice, and when the underside is browned (about 7 to 8 minutes), turn and grill the other side, basting once or twice, and cooking about 8 minutes longer or until flesh of fish separates when tested with a fork. Melt butter in a large metal or flameproof serving platter and transfer fish onto it. In a small bowl mix together the parsley, shallots, and tarragon. Bring fish and herb mixture to the table. Heat Pernod in a small metal pan with a long handle, ignite, and pour flaming over the fish. Sprinkle fish with herbs.
Makes 8 servings

LEMON TARRAGON BUTTER Melt 1/4 cup (50 ml) butter and add 3 tablespoons (45 ml) fresh lemon juice, 1/2 teaspoon (2 ml) salt, 1-1/2 teaspoons (7 ml) minced fresh tarragon or 1/2 teaspoon (2 ml) crushed dried tarragon, and 1 teaspoon (5 ml) grated lemon peel.

SKEWERED SWORDFISH

A colorful seafood kebab reminiscent of Aegean cookery. Those who have access to bay (laurel) trees can use the leaves to give added flavor to this dish; soak leaves in water first to avoid charring.

3 tablespoons (45 ml) olive oil
1/2 cup (125 ml) dry white wine or vermouth
2 tablespoons (30 ml) fresh lemon juice
1/2 teaspoon (2 ml) salt
1-1/2 teaspoons (7 ml) chopped fresh oregano, or
    1/2 teaspoon (2 ml) crushed dried oregano
1 garlic clove, minced
1-1/3 pounds (650 g) swordfish, shark, or halibut steaks, cut 3/4-inch (2 cm) thick
12 cherry tomatoes
12 fresh bay (laurel) leaves, soaked in water (optional)
1 lemon, cut in wedges
Crushed fresh or dried oregano

Mix together in a bowl the oil, wine, lemon juice, salt, oregano, and garlic. Cut fish steaks into 1-1/4-inch (4 cm) squares, removing skin and bones, and place in oil mixture. Cover and chill several hours, turning several times. Drain fish and alternate on skewers with tomatoes and bay leaves. Place over hot coals or under a broiler for about 10 minutes, turning to brown both sides and basting with marinade until flesh of fish separates when tested with a fork. Accompany with lemon wedges and a small bowl of oregano to sprinkle over.
Makes 4 servings

CHARCOAL-GRILLED FISH IN GRAPE LEAVES

In Provence, small fish such as the Mediterranean red mullet are marinated in fennel and Pernod, wrapped in a dampened grape leaf, and grilled briefly over charcoal. The charred leaf is then unwrapped and discarded, leaving a moist and aromatic fish.

6 small whole sanddabs, fresh sardines, or smelt (3 to 4 ounces or 75 to 125 g each)
1/4 cup (50 ml) olive oil
1/4 cup (50 ml) minced fresh fennel leaves (optional)
1 tablespoon (15 ml) Pernod
Fresh grape leaves, soaked in water
Lemon wedges

Marinate fish in a mixture of the oil, fennel, and Pernod for at least 1 hour. Wrap each fish in one or two dampened grape leaves. Grill over hot coals, turning once, cooking about 2 minutes on each side. Serve accompanied with lemon wedges.
Makes 6 small servings

FISH IN A SPRING CLOAK

A broiled mushroom, Gruyère cheese, and *crème fraîche* topping masks fish that is first poached and then broiled.

1-1/3 pounds (650 g) turbot, sole, ono, red snapper, or other white-fleshed fish fillets
1/2 cup (125 ml) dry white wine or vermouth
Salt and white pepper
2 green onions, chopped
3 tablespoons (45 ml) chopped parsley
8 ounces (250 g) mushrooms, sliced
1 tablespoon (15 ml) butter
4 tablespoons (60 ml) Crème Fraîche, page 116, or sour cream
4 ounces (125 g) Gruyère or Jarlsberg cheese, shredded (about 1 cup or 250 ml)
2 tomatoes, cut into wedges

In a large frying pan, poach fish fillets in wine with salt, pepper, and 1 tablespoon (15 ml) each of the onions and parsley until half cooked, about 4 minutes. Transfer to a flameproof platter. Boil down pan juices until reduced to 2 tablespoons (30 ml). Spoon pan juices over fish and place under a broiler until flesh of fish separates when tested with a fork, about 2 minutes longer. It will take on a lightly browned sheen. In another large frying pan, sauté mushrooms in butter with remaining onion and parsley for 1 minute. Stir in Crème Fraîche and half the cheese. Spoon over fish. Arrange tomato wedges around the sides of the fish. Sprinkle remaining cheese on top and place under a broiler until cheese melts.

Makes 4 servings

BROILED TURBOT WITH TAHINI

Armenian restaurateur Aram Janjigian shares his superb way of glorifying fish: broiled with garlic butter and served with a sauce of *tahini,* mint, and lemon juice.

1 pound (500 g) turbot, sole, or red
    snapper fillets
Salt and white pepper
2 tablespoons (30 ml) butter
2 garlic cloves, minced
3 tablespoons (45 ml) *tahini**
1/4 cup (50 ml) fresh lemon juice
2 tablespoons (30 ml) chopped
    fresh mint
Mint sprigs

Place fish on a broiling pan and season with salt and pepper. Melt butter with garlic and drizzle over fish. Place under a broiler and broil on one side only, until fish is golden brown and flesh separates when tested with a fork. Transfer to a heated platter. Mix together the *tahini,* lemon juice, and chopped mint and spoon over fish. Garnish with mint sprigs.

Makes 3 to 4 servings

*Ground sesame seed paste, available in health food stores and Middle Eastern markets.

FISH CREOLE STYLE

A spicy tomato sauce laden with shrimp and mushrooms blankets fish in a dish from the American South.

1/2 cup (125 ml) minced onion
1/4 cup (50 ml) chopped green or red
    bell pepper
3 tablespoons (45 ml) butter
4 ounces (125 g) mushrooms, thinly
    sliced
2 medium tomatoes, peeled, seeded,
    and chopped, or
    1 can (8 ounces or 225 g) tomato
    sauce
1/2 teaspoon (2 ml) each chili powder,
    ground cumin, and ground
    coriander
4 ounces (125 g) cooked small shrimp
Salt and freshly ground black pepper
1 pound (500 g) turbot, sea bass,
    orange roughy, or sole fillets
Salt and freshly ground black pepper
Fresh coriander sprigs

In a large frying pan sauté onion and pepper in 2 tablespoons (30 ml) of the butter until glazed. Add mushrooms and sauté 1 minute. Add tomatoes, chili powder, cumin, and ground coriander and simmer 5 minutes. Add shrimp, salt, and pepper and heat through. Place fish fillets on a broiling pan. Season with salt and pepper and

dot with remaining butter. Place under a broiler until browned and flesh of fish separates when tested with a fork, about 5 minutes. Place broiled fish on a heated platter, stir fish juices from the broiling pan into the sauce, and spoon sauce over fish. Garnish with fresh coriander.

Makes 4 servings

BROILED KING CRAB LEGS

The succulent meat of the Alaska King crab is superb when basted with butter and broiled.

2 King crab legs (about 1-1/2 pounds
    or 750 g)
2 tablespoons (30 ml) butter, melted
1/4 cup (50 ml) each yogurt and sour
    cream
1 shallot or green onion (white part
    only), chopped
1 tablespoon (15 ml) minced parsley
1 lemon, cut in wedges

Break crab legs at the joints (use gloves to protect your hands). With scissors, cut down the sides of shells and lift off the upper half of each shell. Arrange crab legs in a baking pan and brush crab meat with melted butter. Place about 5 inches (13 cm) below the broiler and broil until heated through, about 5 minutes. Mix together yogurt, sour cream, shallot, and parsley and serve as a sauce alongside. Garnish with lemon wedges.

Makes 2 to 3 servings

Poached & Steamed Fish

POACHING AND STEAMING

Poaching is a flavorful, low-calorie cooking technique that can be used for almost any kind of fish, whether filleted, cut in steaks, or whole. ("Boiled" lobster, crab, and shrimp are actually poached in simmering liquid, not boiled.) Poaching is a particularly good method of cooking delicate, mild-flavored fish such as sole. To poach, place the fish in a flameproof container and barely cover the fish with a liquid such as wine, court bouillon, or stock; if you like, chopped vegetables may be added to the container to help flavor the fish. For large fish, a fish poacher, which contains a perforated rack used to lift the fish out of its cooking liquid, is ideal (brush the rack with oil or melted butter before adding the fish). Without a poacher, wrap the fish in cheesecloth, with long strings tied at each end to aid in lifting the fish out of the liquid, and cook in a large kettle or Dutch oven. Fish is poached at a gentle simmer on top of the stove until the flesh of the fish separates when tested with a fork. Poached fish may be served hot or chilled. The poaching liquid may be reduced and used as a basis for a sauce, if you like.

Fish may also be oven-poached, or braised, in which case it is usually half-covered with liquid and the container is loosely covered with parchment, wax paper; or aluminum foil with a small hole cut in it for the steam to escape. Cook in a preheated 350°F (180°C) oven until the flesh of the fish separates when tested with a fork.

The Oriental technique of steaming foods above boiling water may also be used for any kind and cut of fish, though it is most commonly used for whole fish. Place the fish in a steamer or in a shallow heatproof container set on a wooden trivet in a covered wok, or improvise a steamer by placing the fish in a shallow heatproof container set on a metal loaf pan or a heatproof bowl in a large, covered kettle (clams and mussels may be placed directly into a small amount of water or other cooking liquid). Seasoning such as soy sauce, ginger, or garlic may be sprinkled over fish before it is steamed, if you like. Watch to see that the water does not boil away, and add more water during the cooking process, if necessary. Also check to see that you have not used too much water—it should not splash up onto the fish.

HALIBUT PORTUGUESE STYLE

A sherried tomato sauce smothers fish steaks in a dish from Portugal.

1-1/4 to 1-1/2 pounds (625 to 750 g) halibut, mahi-mahi, or sea bass steaks
Salt and freshly ground black pepper
2 tablespoons (30 ml) fresh lemon juice
1 medium onion, minced
2 garlic cloves, minced
3 tablespoons (45 ml) olive oil
1 large tomato, peeled, seeded, and chopped
3 tablespoons (45 ml) tomato paste
1/4 cup (50 ml) chopped parsley
1/2 teaspoon (2 ml) brown sugar
1/2 cup (125 ml) each dry sherry and water
1 lemon, sliced
1 tablespoon (15 ml) butter

Place fish in a buttered shallow baking dish and season with salt and pepper and sprinkle with lemon juice. In a saucepan sauté onion and garlic in oil until soft. Add tomato, tomato paste, parsley, sugar, sherry, and water and simmer until blended. Pour sauce over fish and arrange lemon slices on top. Dot with butter. Cover dish with aluminum foil and bake in a preheated 375°F (190°C) oven for 25 to 30 minutes or until flesh of fish separates when tested with a fork.
Makes 4 servings

HALIBUT WITH GREEN PEPPERCORN SAUCE

A rich sauce with sprightly peppercorns smothers fish steaks.

1 tablespoon (15 ml) fresh lemon juice
1/2 teaspoon (2 ml) salt
1 garlic clove, minced
1-1/2 pounds (750 g) halibut or
    swordfish steaks
1 garlic clove, minced
3 tablespoons (45 ml) butter
3 medium tomatoes, peeled, seeded,
    and chopped
2 tablespoons (30 ml) drained canned
    green peppercorns (or to taste)
1 tablespoon (15 ml) Dijon-style
    mustard
1/4 cup (50 ml) dry white wine
2/3 cup (150 ml) heavy cream
2 tablespoons (30 ml) brandy or
    cognac

Mix lemon, salt, and garlic together and spread on fish; set aside. In a large frying pan melt butter, add tomatoes, peppercorns, mustard, and wine and cook, stirring frequently, for 5 minutes or until thick. Place fish in pan, reduce heat, and cook for 6 to 8 minutes on each side or until flesh of fish separates when tested with a fork. Transfer fish to a hot platter and keep warm. Add cream and brandy to the sauce and cook, stirring, for 5 minutes or until blended and thickened. Spoon over fish.
Makes 4 servings

SHAD ROE WITH SORREL

Sorrel has a slightly tart taste that combines well with shad roe. It is worthwhile to grow a pot of sorrel from seed if it is not readily available in the market. Watercress is an acceptable substitute in this recipe.

2 shallots or green onions (white part
    only), minced
2 tablespoons (30 ml) butter
1/2 cup (125 ml) chopped fresh sorrel
1 cup (250 ml) dry white wine or
    vermouth
3 pairs shad roe
Salt, white pepper, and freshly grated
    nutmeg
3/4 cup (175 ml) heavy cream

In a large frying pan sauté shallots in butter until soft. Scatter sorrel over the shallots and pour in wine. Arrange roe on top and season with salt, pepper, and nutmeg. Cover, bring to a boil, and simmer 15 minutes, or until roe is cooked through. Transfer roe to a heated platter with a slotted spoon and keep warm. Bring pan juices to a boil, add cream, and cook down until reduced to a saucelike consistency. Spoon over roe.
Makes 3 to 4 servings

ORIENTAL STEAMED FISH

A whole fish steamed Chinese style excels in its simplicity. Threads of scallions and ginger blanket it, then smoking hot oil is poured over and a ladleful of soy sauce melds the flavors. From the deft hands of beloved Chef Louis Kao.

One 2- to 2-1/2- pound (1 to 1.25 kg)
    whole rockfish or sea bass
5 green onions (white parts only)
2-1/2-inch (6 cm) piece ginger root
1/3 cup (75 ml) cottonseed or
    safflower oil
1/3 cup (75 ml) soy sauce
Fresh coriander sprigs

Slash fish lengthwise at the thickest part on both sides so that it cooks evenly. Lay fish on a metal platter and place it inside a steamer over boiling water. Cover and steam about 15 minutes, or until flesh of fish separates when tested with a fork. Remove from the steamer and drain off all liquid in platter. Meanwhile, shred onion into fine lengthwise shreds. Peel ginger and cut into fine lengthwise pieces. Scatter onions and ginger over fish. Heat oil almost to the smoking point and pour it over the garnished fish, then spoon soy sauce over all. Garnish with fresh coriander.
Makes 4 to 6 servings

SALMON IN CHAMPAGNE SAUCE

A broiled cream and champagne sauce makes a royal cloak for salmon.

One 2- to 2-1/2-pound (1 to 1.5 kg) salmon fillet, skinned
1 tomato, peeled, seeded, and sliced
4 medium mushrooms, sliced
1 shallot or green onion (white part only), minced
Salt, white pepper, and minced fresh or crushed dried tarragon to taste
2 cups (500 ml) champagne
1 cup (250 ml) heavy cream
4 tablespoons (60 ml) butter
Watercress sprigs

Arrange fillet in a buttered baking dish and scatter tomato, mushrooms, and shallot over it. Season with salt, pepper, and tarragon. Pour champagne over. Cover dish with aluminum foil and cook in a preheated 375°F (190°C) oven for 8 to 10 minutes or until flesh of fish separates when tested with a fork. Transfer fish to a flameproof serving platter and keep warm. Pour pan juices and vegetables into a blender or a food processor fitted with a steel blade and purée until smooth. Pour into a frying pan and boil down until reduced by half. Add cream and reduce further to a saucelike consistency. Swirl in 1 tablespoon (15 ml) of the butter at a time, heating just until blended in. Coat fish with the sauce and place under a broiler until lightly browned. Serve any remaining sauce alongside. Garnish with watercress.
Makes 6 servings

POACHED SALMON WITH SAUCE VERTE

A Parisian friend and cooking teacher, Erna Jacquillat, shares a marvelous recipe for cold poached fish with a verdant herb mayonnaise.

1 onion, sliced
1 carrot, sliced
1 tablespoon (15 ml) crushed dried thyme
2 bay leaves
1 bunch parsley
2 garlic cloves
1-1/2 teaspoons (7 ml) peppercorns
1-1/2 tablespoons (25 ml) rock salt
3 tablespoons (45 ml) red wine vinegar
One 4-pound (2 kg) whole salmon, or 4 to 6 medium trout
3 to 4 carrots, cut into very thin crosswise slices
Watercress sprigs
Lemon wedges or slices
Sauce Verte, following

In a fish poacher or a soup pot large enough to accommodate the fish place the onion, carrot, thyme, bay leaves, parsley, garlic, peppercorns, rock salt, wine vinegar, and add water to a depth equal to the thickness of the fish. Bring to a boil and simmer 20 minutes. Add salmon or trout and simmer salmon 15 minutes, trout 7 to 8 minutes. Remove fish, drain, and cool. Peel skin from fish, leaving head and tail intact, if possible. Decorate with sliced carrots to simulate scales, and garnish with watercress and lemon. Pass a bowl of Sauce Verte alongside, or mask fish with Sauce Verte before decorating.
Makes 4 to 6 servings

SAUCE VERTE Place 1 egg yolk in a bowl or blender. Mix in 1-1/2 teaspoons (7 ml) Dijon-style mustard and 1/2 teaspoon (2 ml) salt. Gradually add 1 cup (250 ml) safflower oil in a thin stream, beating with a whisk or blending until smooth and thick. Add 3 tablespoons (45 ml) fresh lemon juice, 1 bunch parsley, minced (about 4 ounces or 125 g), and 1/4 cup (50 ml) minced watercress or 2 tablespoons (30 ml) minced fresh tarragon. Makes about 2 cups (500 ml).

SNAPPER ROMAN STYLE

A renowned Italian way with fish is this one emphasizing anchovies and mushrooms.

1/3 cup (75 ml) chopped onion
3 tablespoons (45 ml) olive oil or
    butter
3 anchovy fillets, rinsed, drained, and
    diced
1 garlic clove, minced
2 tablespoons (30 ml) chopped parsley
1-1/2 pounds (750 g) red snapper,
    monkfish, or sea bass
Salt and freshly ground black pepper
1 cup (250 ml) dry white wine or
    vermouth
1/4 cup (50 ml) water
4 ounces (125 g) mushrooms, sliced
1 teaspoon (5 ml) cornstarch blended
    with
1 tablespoon (15 ml) cold water

In a large frying pan sauté onion in 1 tablespoon (15 ml) of the oil. Add anchovies, garlic, and 1 tablespoon (15 ml) of the parsley and cook, stirring, 1 minute. Push to the sides of the pan. Add 1 tablespoon (15 ml) of the oil and sauté fish, turning to brown both sides. Season with salt and pepper. Pour in wine and water, bring to a boil, cover, and simmer 10 minutes, or until flesh of fish separates when tested with a fork. Meanwhile, heat remaining oil in another pan and sauté mushrooms and remaining parsley for 1 minute. Transfer fish to a heated platter and keep warm. Stir fish juices into mushrooms. Bring to a boil and stir in cornstarch paste; cook until thickened and spoon over fish.
Makes 6 servings

POACHED FISH IN ALMOND-CHILI SAUCE

A favorite Mexican recipe for snapper uses green husk tomatoes, marketed in this country as tomatillos.

1 cup (250 ml) dry white wine or
    vermouth
1 can (10 ounces or 284 g) tomatillos
1 large onion, sliced
1 garlic clove, minced
Dash salt and freshly ground black
    pepper
One 3-pound (1.5 kg) chunk red
    snapper, sea bass, monkfish, or
    other firm, white-fleshed fish
3 tablespoons (45 ml) sesame seeds
1/2 cup (125 ml) each blanched
    almonds and walnuts
2 canned peeled green chili peppers
Fresh coriander sprigs
1 lemon, cut in wedges

In a large saucepan or fish poacher combine wine, liquid from canned tomatillos, onion, garlic, salt, and pepper. Bring to a boil and simmer 15 minutes. Add fish and poach 15 minutes, or until flesh of fish separates when tested with a fork. Transfer to a heated platter; keep warm. Toast sesame seeds by stirring in a heated ungreased frying pan until lightly browned, taking care not to burn them; set aside. Pour poaching liquid into a blender along with onion, then add tomatillos, nuts, sesame seeds, and peppers and blend to a smooth purée. Place in a saucepan and heat thoroughly but do not allow to boil. Spoon some of sauce over fish and pass remaining sauce alongside. Garnish fish with fresh coriander and lemon wedges.

Makes 6 to 8 servings

SOLE DUGLÉRÉ

This is an easy, French family-style dish.

4 sole, turbot, whiting, orange roughy, or other white-fleshed fish fillets (about 1-1/4 pounds or 625 g)
Salt and white pepper
2 tablespoons (30 ml) butter
2 shallots or green onions (white part only), chopped
1 garlic clove, minced
1/3 cup (75 ml) Fish Stock, page 115, or clam juice
1/3 cup (75 ml) dry white wine or vermouth
1 large tomato, peeled, seeded, and chopped
1 tablespoon (15 ml) butter
2 tablespoons (30 ml) chopped parsley

Season fish fillets with salt and pepper, roll up, and secure with toothpicks. In a large frying pan sauté shallots and garlic in butter until soft. Add Fish Stock, wine, and tomato and bring to a boil. Arrange fish in pan, cover, and simmer 10 to 12 minutes, or until flesh of fish separates when tested with a fork. Remove fish to a heated platter and keep warm. Bring sauce to a boil and reduce slightly, then swirl in butter. Spoon over fish and sprinkle with parsley.

Makes 4 servings

SOLE VÉRONIQUE

Tart-sweet seedless green grapes lend sparkle to a delicate wine sauce on fish fillets.

4 sole, whiting, or turbot fillets (about
    1-1/4 pounds or 625 g)
Salt and white pepper
1-1/2 tablespoons (25 ml) fresh lime
    or lemon juice
1/2 cup (125 ml) dry white wine or
    vermouth
1 tablespoon (15 ml) butter
1 cup (250 ml) seedless grapes
2 teaspoons (10 ml) cornstarch
    blended with
1 tablespoon (15 ml) cold water
1 tablespoon (15 ml) Cointreau,
    curaçao, or other orange-flavored
    liqueur, or undiluted orange juice
    concentrate
3 tablespoons (45 ml) heavy cream
Lime or lemon wedges

Season fish fillets with salt and pepper and sprinkle with lime juice. Place in a frying pan, add wine, and bring to a boil and simmer, covered, for about 6 minutes, or until flesh of fish separates when tested with a fork. Transfer to a heated platter and keep warm. Melt butter in a saucepan, add grapes and heat, shaking pan, until grapes are heated through. With a slotted spoon, spoon grapes over fish. Pour wine juices into butter in pan and bring to a boil. Stir in cornstarch paste. Stirring, cook until thickened. Blend in liqueur and cream and heat through. Pour sauce over fish and grapes and garnish with lime wedges.
Makes 4 servings

SOLE STUFFED WITH SHRIMP QUENELLES

Shrimp dumplings poached in a wheel of fish.

8 ounces (250 g) medium shrimp in
    the shell
1 cup (250 ml) water
1/4 teaspoon (1 ml) salt
2 tablespoons (30 ml) butter
1 teaspoon (5 ml) fresh lemon juice
1/2 cup (125 ml) all-purpose flour
2 egg yolks
Poaching Liquid, following
6 sole or flounder fillets (about 1-1/2
    pounds or 750 g)
Hollandaise Sauce, page 124

Shell and devein shrimp, reserving shells. Place shrimp in a blender with water and blend until minced. Drain, reserving liquid. Combine salt, butter, reserved liquid, and lemon juice in a saucepan and bring to a boil. Remove from heat and add flour all at once. Stir vigorously until flour is absorbed and a thick mixture results. Allow to cool 5 minutes, then beat in egg yolks and shrimp and refrigerate until well chilled, about 1 hour. Meanwhile, prepare Poaching Liquid and let cool. Turn chilled shrimp mixture out onto a lightly floured surface; shape into a small log and cut into 6 equal portions. Place 1 portion of shrimp mixture on each piece of fish. Roll and secure with a toothpick. Place cool Poaching Liquid in a large frying pan with a cover and add stuffed fish fillets. Bring to a simmer, cover, and cook for 15 minutes or until fish is opaque throughout and flesh separates when tested with a fork. Remove from broth and serve with Hollandaise Sauce.
Makes 6 servings

POACHING LIQUID In a saucepan sauté 1/2 carrot, sliced, and 1 sliced onion in 1 tablespoon (15 ml) butter. Add reserved shrimp shells from above recipe and cook until red. Add 1 cup (250 ml) clam juice, 1 cup (250 ml) dry white wine or vermouth, 1/4 cup (50 ml) chopped parsley, and 1 bay leaf. Simmer 30 minutes, uncovered. Strain and let cool to room temperature.

FISH DOLMAS

The Greek method of wrapping vegetables in grape leaves also works remarkably well for fish. The leaves have a piquant flavor and are eaten together with the fish. Without grape leaves, substitute Swiss chard or spinach leaves.

1 pound (500 g) turbot, cod, whiting, or sole fillets
Salt and freshly ground black pepper
1-1/2 teaspoons (7 ml) chopped fresh oregano or basil, or
  1/2 teaspoon (2 ml) crushed dried oregano or basil
4 large grape leaves, packed in brine, or
  4 large fresh grape leaves, blanched in boiling water 4 minutes
1/2 cup (125 ml) Fish Stock, page 115, or clam juice
1/4 cup (50 ml) dry white wine or vermouth
1 tablespoon (15 ml) pine nuts or pistachios, chopped
1 teaspoon (5 ml) cornstarch mixed with
1 tablespoon (15 ml) cold water

Cut fish into 4 serving pieces and season with salt, pepper, and oregano. Wrap each in a grape leaf. Pour Fish Stock and wine into a frying pan, arrange wrapped fish in pan seam side down and bring to a simmer. Cover and cook 5 to 6 minutes or until flesh of fish separates when tested with a fork. Meanwhile, if using pine nuts, toast them by placing them in a baking pan in a preheated 325°F (160°C) oven for 8 to 10 minutes or until lightly toasted. Transfer fish to a heated platter. Stir cornstarch paste into pan juices and bring to a boil; stirring, cook until thickened. Spoon sauce into a bowl to serve alongside fish. Garnish fish with nuts and lemon slices.
Makes 4 servings

WHITING FILLETS BONNE FEMME

In French cooking, *bonne femme* signifies that the good wife included mushrooms in the dish.

2 shallots or green onions (white part only), chopped
4 ounces (125 g) mushrooms, sliced
1 tablespoon (15 ml) butter
1 to 1-1/4 pounds (500 to 625 g) whiting, sole, or turbot fillets
Salt and white pepper
3/4 cup (175 ml) dry white wine or vermouth
1/4 cup (50 ml) heavy cream
2 tablespoons (30 ml) each minced chives and parsley

In a large frying pan sauté shallots and mushrooms in butter for 1 minute. Arrange fish fillets on top and season with salt and pepper. Pour in wine and cover and simmer for 10 minutes, or until flesh of fish separates when tested with a fork. Transfer to a heated platter and keep warm. Add cream to pan juices and cook down until reduced by half. Spoon over fish and sprinkle with chives and parsley.
Makes 4 servings

CRACKED CRAB

There's no better way to celebrate the opening of Dungeness crab season each year than a supper of chilled crab, melted sweet butter or homemade mayonnaise, French sourdough bread, and a crisp Johannisberg Riesling or Sauvignon Blanc.

Live Dungeness crabs* (about 1 pound
    or 500 g per person)
Melted unsalted butter and/or one
    or more sauces (see below)

In a large kettle bring to a boil enough water to generously cover crabs and add about 1 tablespoon (15 ml) salt for each quart (1 L) of water. Add crabs and cook 8 minutes per pound. Remove and plunge into cold water; drain and allow to cool. Clean and crack as directed on page 15. To serve, mound crab sections on a platter and accompany with melted butter in individual dishes, or serve with one or more sauces such as Mayonnaise, Skordalia, Aioli, Green Mayonnaise, or Remoulade (see Stocks and Sauces).

*If you prefer, kill the crabs just before boiling: Place a crab on its back on a cutting board and hold a large chef's knife or cleaver blade down in the center of the crab; hit the knife sharply with a hammer.

STEAMED CLAMS

Melted butter sparked with lime juice makes a succulent dipping sauce for steamed clams.

3 pounds (1.5 kg) small hard-shelled
    clams
1/2 cup (125 ml) dry white wine or
    vermouth
2 tablespoons (30 ml) butter
1 garlic clove, minced
1/2 pound (250 g) unsalted butter,
    melted
1 lime, cut into wedges

Soak clams in salted water for 30 minutes (see page 16). Scrub clams well under cold running water with a stiff-bristled brush. Pour wine into a steamer, large pan, or soup pot and add butter, garlic, and clams. Cover and steam just until shells open, about 6 to 10 minutes. Discard any clams that do not open. Arrange clams, still in their shells, in shallow soup bowls and pour broth over them. Pour melted butter into small dishes and serve alongside. Garnish each butter dish with a lime wedge.
*Makes 6 first-course servings or
3 to 4 entrée servings*

BOILED LOBSTER

Savor boiled lobster hot or chilled, with melted butter or a sauce.

Live Northern lobsters* (about
    1 pound or 500 g per person)
Melted unsalted butter and/or one or
    more sauces (see below)

In a large kettle, bring to a boil enough water to generously cover lobsters and add about 1 tablespoon (15 ml) salt for each quart (1 L) of water. Wearing gloves, grasp body of each lobster behind the large front claws or front legs. Plunge headfirst into boiling water, bring water back to a simmer, then cover and cook about 7 minutes for a 1-pound (500 g) lobster or 10 minutes for a 2-pound (1 kg) lobster. Remove and plunge into cold water; drain. Clean and crack as directed on page 16. Serve hot with individual bowls of melted butter or chilled with a sauce such as Mayonnaise, Aioli, Green Mayonnaise, or Tapenade (see Stocks and Sauces).

*If you prefer, kill the lobsters just before cooking by piercing them with a large knife in the underside, close to the chest.

STEAMED MUSSELS

One of the best ways to cook mussels is also the simplest: Steam them in garlic butter until the shells open, savor them out of hand with crusty French sourdough bread to dip up the nectarlike juices, and sip a crisp Johannisberg Riesling. If you are adventurous enough, garner mussels (in season only; see page 132) by the ocean at low tide and cook them there. Pure ecstacy: amid the salt air, with family and friends, on a minus tide day in a secret spot on the shore.

3 quarts (3 L) mussels in the shell
   (about 4 pounds or 2 kg)
3 garlic cloves, minced
6 shallots or green onions (white part
   only), chopped
3 tablespoons (50 ml) olive oil or
   butter
1 cup (250 ml) dry white wine or
   vermouth
1/3 cup (75 ml) minced parsley
Freshly ground black pepper
Melted butter (optional)

Soak mussels for 30 minutes in salted water (see page 16). Scrub mussels well under cold running water with a stiff-bristled brush. In a large soup kettle sauté garlic and shallots in oil until soft, stirring occasionally. Add wine, parsley, and pepper, and bring to a boil. Add mussels, cover, and simmer gently until the shells open, about 8 minutes; discard any that do not open. Spoon mussels into individual soup bowls and ladle broth over them. Pass butter, if desired, for dipping the mussels in.
Makes about 12 first-course servings or 3 to 4 entrée servings

PORTUGUESE MARINER'S PLATTER

In the seaport town of Cascais, Portugal, a huge platter of butter-steeped shellfish is the specialty of O Pipas, a stunning modern restaurant. There each stainless-steel platter for two comes heaped with several dozen tiny clams, coral mussels, delectable crayfish, and big shrimp with popping black eyes. Here, select your shellfish from the choices available in the marketplace.

2 pounds (1 kg) small hard-shelled
   clams or mussels
12 jumbo shrimp in the shell
2 rock lobster tails, cooked and split,
   or
   1 Dungeness crab, cooked, cleaned,
   and cracked
1 cup (250 ml) dry white wine or
   vermouth
1 shallot or green onion (white part
   only), chopped
6 tablespoons (90 ml) minced
   parsley or fresh coriander
2 garlic cloves, minced
1/4 pound (125 g) unsalted butter
Lemon wedges

Soak clams in salted water for 30 minutes (see page 16), and scrub under cold running water with a stiff-bristled brush. Place clams, shrimp, and lobster in a large kettle with wine, shallot, 4 tablespoons (60 ml) of the parsley, and garlic. Cover and simmer for 5 to 10 minutes, or until clam shells open; discard any clams that do not open. Transfer shellfish to a large, heated platter. Melt butter and add remaining parsley, then spoon over shellfish. Garnish with lemon wedges.
Makes 4 servings

SHRIMP IN WINE

The Northern Italian technique of simmering shrimp in a vegetable-flavored wine broth makes a choice dish that can be served hot, accompanied with fresh pasta, or cold with Pesto Mayonnaise.

1 cup (250 ml) each water and dry
    white wine or vermouth
1/3 cup (75 ml) each thinly sliced
    onion, carrot, and celery
1/3 cup (75 ml) thinly sliced leek,
    white part only (optional)
2 parsley sprigs
1 bay leaf
1 teaspoon (5 ml) chopped fresh
    thyme, or
    1/4 teaspoon (1 ml) crushed dried
    thyme
1/2 teaspoon (2 ml) salt
4 peppercorns
2 pounds (1 kg) large shrimp in the
    shell
Pesto Mayonnaise, page 119

In a large pan simmer the water, wine, onion, carrot, celery, leek, parsley, bay leaf, thyme, salt, and peppercorns for 15 minutes. Add the shrimp and simmer, covered, for 4 to 5 minutes, or until they turn pink. Serve hot, in the shell, or chill and serve in the shell with Pesto Mayonnaise.
Makes 4 servings

CHINESE FIREPOT WITH SEAFOOD

A firepot is a convivial entrée for a group of intimate friends.

8 ounces (250 g) squid
8 ounces (250 g) sole or orange roughy
    fillets, thinly sliced crosswise
8 ounces (250 g) shrimp, shelled and
    deveined
8 ounces (250 g) sea scallops, sliced
    or quartered
1 eggplant, peeled and cubed
1 bunch green onions, cut in 1-inch
    (3 cm) lengths
12 dried Chinese mushrooms,
    soaked, or
    4 ounces (125 g) button mush-
    rooms
About 6 cups (1.5 L) chicken broth or
    consommé
Soy sauce
Chili sauce

Clean squid (see page 17) and cut in thin crosswise slices. Arrange squid, sole, shrimp, scallops, and vegetables on a platter. Half fill a Chinese firepot or electric saucepot with chicken broth and place on the table. Heat to simmering. Provide each diner with individual dishes of soy sauce and chili sauce for dipping. Let each person skewer his choice of ingredients with a bamboo skewer and hold it in the simmering stock until cooked through. The cooked food is then dipped into the sauces.
Makes 4 to 6 servings

PICKLED SHRIMP SWEDISH STYLE

For a summer picnic or sailing outing, a crock of subtly spiced shrimp is perfect with dark rye bread, cherry tomatoes, and pickles.

1/4 cup (50 ml) celery leaves
1 tablespoon (15 ml) pickling spices,
    tied in a small square of cheesecloth
1 teaspoon (5 ml) salt
2 cups (500 ml) water
1 pound (500 g) medium to large
    shrimp in the shell
2/3 cup (150 ml) safflower oil
1/3 cup (75 ml) white wine vinegar
1 teaspoon (5 ml) celery seed
Salt and freshly ground black pepper
1 tablespoon (15 ml) capers
1 small onion, thinly sliced
2 bay leaves

Place in a large saucepan the celery leaves, pickling spice, salt, and water; bring to a boil and simmer 10 minutes. Add shrimp and simmer 5 minutes, or until shrimp turn pink. Drain and let cool. Shell and devein shrimp. In a bowl combine the oil, vinegar, celery seed, salt, pepper, and capers. In a crock or other wide-mouthed jar, alternate shrimp, onion slices, and bay leaves and pour oil and vinegar mixture over. Cover and chill at least 1 day for flavors to blend.
Makes 4 to 6 servings

Baked Fish

BAKING

Baking is a cooking method that is suitable for almost all fish. Use a lightly oiled ovenproof dish or pan and, if you like, strew the dish with a layer of cut-up vegetables such as carrots, onions, celery, and leeks. (The vegetables may first be lightly sautéed in butter, or the raw vegetables may be dotted with butter in the dish.) Lay the fish—whole, cut in steaks, or filleted—on top. Brush the surface of the fish with oil and/or melted butter, or baste once or twice during baking with broth or wine. Season the fish lightly with salt and white pepper. Bake uncovered in a preheated 425° to 450°F (220° to 230°C) oven for 10 minutes per inch (3 cm) of the thickness of the fish, or about 8 to 10 minutes per pound. The fish is done when the flesh of the fish separates when tested with a fork and the juices of the fish are just beginning to exude. Note: Casseroles and gratins are usually cooked at a lower temperature of 350° to 375°F (160° to 180°C) —see Casseroles and Gratins for specific recipes.

BAKED HALIBUT
WITH VEGETABLES

Yaya, my mother-in-law, is a specialist at cooking fish Greek style. In this recipe she sandwiches fish steaks between spinach and other vegetables and herbs. As the fish bakes, it absorbs a superb garden flavor, and the vegetables acquire an almost caramelized sweetness.

2 bunches green onions, chopped
1/4 cup (50 ml) olive oil
3 stalks celery, minced
3 carrots, thinly sliced
1 large bunch spinach (about 1 pound or 500 g), chopped
1/2 cup (125 ml) minced parsley
2 tomatoes, peeled, seeded, and diced
4 mint leaves, chopped (optional)
2 garlic cloves, minced
Salt and freshly ground black pepper
2 pounds (1 kg) halibut, mahi-mahi, swordfish, shark, or sea bass steaks, cut 1-inch (3 cm) thick
1 lemon, cut in wedges

In a large frying pan sauté onions in oil until soft. Add celery, carrots, spinach, parsley, tomatoes, mint, garlic, salt, and pepper. Cover and simmer 15 minutes. Spoon half of the vegetable mixture into a buttered baking pan, cover with the fish steaks, and spoon remaining vegetable mixture on top. Cover and bake in a preheated 350°F (180°C) oven for 45 minutes, or until flesh of fish separates when tested with a fork. Serve with lemon wedges.
Makes 6 to 8 servings

BAKED FISH WITH
LEMON BUTTER SAUCE

A young Parisian cooking teacher shares her zestful, easy way of cooking fish.

1 teaspoon (5 ml) fennel seed
One 3-pound (1.5 kg) whole red snapper, rockfish, striped bass or other white-fleshed fish
Salt and white pepper
Lemon Butter Sauce, following

Tuck fennel inside fish. Place fish in a baking pan, sprinkle with salt and pepper, and bake in a preheated 400°F (210°C) oven for 30 minutes, or until flesh of fish separates when tested with a fork. Remove to a heated platter, reserving pan juices. Prepare Lemon Butter Sauce, following, and serve sauce alongside fish.
Makes 6 servings

LEMON BUTTER SAUCE Mix 1/4 pound (125 g) softened unsalted butter with 1-1/2 tablespoons (25 ml) fresh lemon juice, and 2 tablespoons (30 ml) heavy cream and beat with a wire whisk or an electric mixer until well blended. Add 1 teaspoon (5 ml) grated lemon peel and salt and white pepper to taste. Beat in reserved pan juices from the baked fish, above. Stir in 1 tablespoon (15 ml) minced parsley. Makes about 1 cup (250 ml).

SPANISH-STYLE FISH WITH ALMOND SAUCE

In the stunning contemporary *parador* in Guadalajara, Spain, almonds and tomatoes are used to enhance fish.

1 garlic clove, minced
1/4 cup (50 ml) blanched almonds or
    pinenuts
3 tablespoons (45 ml) olive oil
1/4 cup (50 ml) minced parsley
2 large onions, minced
3 medium tomatoes, peeled, seeded,
    and diced, or
    1 can (16 ounces or 450 g) Italian
    plum tomatoes or tomato purée
Salt and freshly ground black pepper
    to taste
1/2 teaspoon (2 ml) sugar
One 1-1/2 pound (750 g) piece of halibut, sea bass, striped bass, or
    red snapper
Salt and freshly ground black pepper

In a frying pan sauté garlic and nuts in 1 tablespoon (15 ml) of the oil until nuts turn golden. Turn out of pan and grind in a mortar or in a blender with parsley and 1 tablespoon (15 ml) of the oil. Sauté onions in remaining oil, cooking until golden. Add tomatoes and simmer 5 to 10 minutes. Stir in nut paste and season with salt, pepper, and sugar. Arrange halibut in a greased shallow baking dish and sprinkle with salt and pepper. Spoon tomato sauce over. Bake in a preheated 375°F (190°C) oven for 20 to 25 minutes or until flesh of fish separates when tested with a fork.
Makes 4 to 5 servings

SALMON AND ASPARAGUS MOUSSELINE

A springtime Swedish treat is fresh asparagus and salmon in hollandaise sauce lightened with whipped cream.

One 2-pound (1 kg) chunk of salmon
Salt and white pepper
12 new potatoes
2 pounds (1 kg) fresh asparagus
Mousseline Sauce, page 125

Place fish on a baking pan and season with salt and pepper. Measure the height of the fish at the thickest part and bake in a preheated 450°F (230°C) oven 10 minutes per inch (3 cm) or until flesh of fish separates when tested with a fork. Remove from oven and place on a heated platter. Meanwhile, cook potatoes in boiling salted water until tender, about 20 minutes. With a small sharp knife, peel asparagus from tip to butt. Cook in boiling salted water until tender-crisp, about 5 to 7 minutes. Flank salmon with asparagus and potatoes and spoon Mousseline Sauce over all. Pass remaining sauce at the table.
Makes 6 servings

SALMON PIROG

A whole salmon wrapped in brioche dough makes a spectacular main course for a summer party. It can be served hot with hollandaise sauce or cold with sour cream, caviar, and lemon wedges. The following streamlined approach uses a no-knead dough that is surprisingly easy to master.

Rich Brioche Dough, following
One 3-1/2-pound (1.75 kg) whole
    salmon
Salt and freshly ground black pepper
6 green onions, chopped
3 tablespoons (45 ml) butter
8 ounces (250 g) button mushrooms
1 tablespoon (15 ml) fresh lemon juice
3 tablespoons (45 ml) chopped parsley
1 egg yolk beaten with
1 tablespoon (15 ml) milk
Parsley or watercress sprigs
Hollandaise Sauce, page 124, or sour
    cream, caviar, and lemon wedges

Prepare Rich Brioche Dough and chill. Remove head and tail of salmon, and cut out backbone (see Preparing Fish for Stuffing, page 15). Place salmon on a baking sheet and measure its thickness to determine baking time. Bake in a preheated 450°F (230°C) oven for 5 minutes per inch (3 cm) of thickness (this is half the time necessary to bake fish completely). Season with salt and pepper. Remove from oven and let cool 5 minutes, then peel off skin. Cover and chill.

Sauté onions in butter until glazed. Add mushrooms and lemon juice and sauté 1 minute. Remove from heat and mix in parsley. Divide chilled brioche dough in half and roll out each half into a fish shape 1 inch (3 cm) larger all around than the whole fish, allowing an extra 2 inches (5 cm) for the tail. Place 1 piece of dough on a lightly buttered baking sheet. Arrange chilled salmon on top and tuck mushroom mixture inside the cavity of the salmon. Top with remaining brioche dough and press edges to seal. With a knife trim dough into a fish shape and score the tail. Slash sides at midpoint for fins and slash at one end for mouth and eye. Snip top crust in several rows

with scissors to simulate scales. Brush entire surface with egg-milk mixture. Chill 10 minutes. Bake in a preheated 425°F (220°C) oven 20 to 25 minutes or until nicely browned. Serve warm or at room temperature on a platter or board. Garnish with parsley sprigs and accompany with Hollandaise Sauce.
Makes about 10 servings

RICH BRIOCHE DOUGH Sprinkle 1 package (2-3/4 teaspoons or 15 ml) dry yeast into 1/2 cup (125 ml) lukewarm water in a large mixing bowl. Let stand until dissolved. Beat 1/4 pound (125 g) softened butter until creamy and then beat in 1 tablespoon (15 ml) sugar, 1/2 teaspoon (2 ml) salt, and 3 eggs. Measure out 2-1/2 cups (625 ml) all-purpose flour and add 1 cup (250 ml) of the flour to the egg mixture and beat until smooth. Mix in the yeast mixture and beat well. Gradually add remaining flour and beat 5 minutes. Do not knead the dough, as it is too soft. Cover bowl with a towel or plastic film and let rise in a warm place until doubled. Stir down and refrigerate 2 hours or overnight before using.

SWEDISH-STYLE SALMON

Carmelized onion rings and a piquant egg sauce accompany baked salmon in traditional Scandinavian home cooking.

2 large onions, thinly sliced
3 tablespoons (45 ml) butter
One 2-pound (1 kg) chunk of salmon
Watercress or parsley sprigs
Egg Sauce, following

In a large frying pan slowly cook onions in butter, stirring occasionally, about 20 minutes or until golden and caramelized. Meanwhile, lay salmon flat in a baking pan and measure the height of the fish at its thickest point. Bake in a preheated 450°F (230°C) oven for 10 minutes per inch (3 cm) or until flesh of fish separates when tested with a fork. Arrange salmon on a heated serving platter and surround with browned onions. Garnish with watercress and pass Egg Sauce to spoon over.
Makes about 6 servings

EGG SAUCE Press 2 hard-cooked egg yolks through a sieve and mix in 1/4 cup (50 ml) sour cream, 1 teaspoon (5 ml) dry mustard, 2 teaspoons (10 ml) sugar, 1 tablespoon (15 ml) white wine vinegar, and salt and freshly ground black pepper to taste. Whip 1/2 cup (125 ml) heavy cream until stiff and fold in.

BAKED SOLE AMANDINE

A leaner version of the traditional amandine style of cooking fish.

1 pound (500 g) sole, orange roughy, or turbot fillets
3 tablespoons (45 ml) butter, melted
1 teaspoon (5 ml) grated lime or lemon peel
1/4 cup (50 ml) fresh lime or lemon juice
1-1/2 teaspoons (7 ml) chopped fresh thyme, or
    1/2 teaspoon (2 ml) crushed dried thyme
3/4 teaspoon (4 ml) salt
1/4 teaspoon (1 ml) white pepper
1/4 cup (50 ml) slivered blanched almonds
Chopped parsley

Place fish in a shallow baking dish. Combine butter, lime peel, lime juice, thyme, salt, and pepper and pour over fish, turning fish once to coat both sides. Sprinkle fish with almonds. Bake in a preheated 450°F (230°C) oven for 10 to 15 minutes, or until flesh of fish separates when tested with a fork. Sprinkle with parsley.
Makes 3 to 4 servings

SNAPPER IN SEAFOOD SAUCE

From the American Northwest comes my sister's everyday baked snapper—festive enough for guests.

6 medium mushrooms, sliced
1 green onion, chopped
1 tablespoon (15 ml) butter
1 cup (250 ml) milk
1 tablespoon (15 ml) cornstarch
1/2 teaspoon (2 ml) salt
Dash freshly grated nutmeg
1/4 cup (50 ml) dry white wine or vermouth
3 to 4 ounces (75 to 125 g) cooked small shrimp
3 to 4 ounces (75 to 125 g) small oysters, cut in half (optional)
1-1/3 pounds (650 g) red snapper, rockfish, turbot, or sole fillets

Sauté mushrooms and onion in butter until soft; set aside. In a saucepan mix together milk, cornstarch, salt, and nutmeg and cook until thickened, stirring occasionally. Stir in wine, shrimp, oysters, and sautéed mushrooms. Arrange fish in a buttered 7- by 11-inch (18 by 28 cm) baking dish. Pour sauce over fish. Bake in a preheated 400°F (210°C) oven for 15 to 25 minutes, or until flesh of fish separates when tested with a fork (the cooking time will depend on the thickness of the fish).
Makes 4 to 5 servings

FISH WITH CRAB SAUCE

A broiled crab topping on baked sole makes a handsome party dish.

1-1/2 pounds (750 g) sole, turbot, or
    snapper fillets
Salt and white pepper
Cornstarch or flour
1/3 cup (75 ml) dry white wine or
    vermouth
1/2 cup (125 ml) light cream
1-1/2 tablespoons (25 ml) each
    butter and flour
Salt and white pepper to taste
1/2 teaspoon (2 ml) dry mustard
6 ounces (175 g) flaked cooked
    crab meat or cooked small shrimp
1/3 cup (75 ml) heavy cream, whipped
1 tablespoon (15 ml) grated Parmesan
    cheese

Season fish with salt and pepper. Dust lightly with cornstarch and place in a buttered shallow pan. Pour wine and light cream over. Bake in a preheated 450°F (230°C) oven for 8 to 10 minutes, or until flesh of fish separates when tested with a fork. Using a slotted spatula, remove fish to a hot ovenproof platter, reserving the poaching liquid. Melt butter and stir in flour; cook and stir 2 minutes, not allowing flour to brown. Stir in the poaching liquid. Cook, stirring, until thickened. Season with salt, pepper, and mustard. Add crab and cook until heated through. Fold in the whipped cream and spoon sauce over the fish. Sprinkle with cheese and place under a broiler until golden brown.
Makes 4 to 6 servings

FILLET OF SOLE FLORENTINE

A French classic: sole and spinach.

1 large bunch spinach (about 1 pound
    or 500 g)
Salt and white pepper to taste
1-1/4 pounds (625 g) sole or turbot
    fillets
2 tablespoons (30 ml) each butter and
    flour
3/4 cup (175 ml) half-and-half
1/4 cup (50 ml) dry white wine or
    vermouth
2 ounces (50 g) Gruyère or Jarlsberg
    cheese, shredded (about 1/2 cup
    or 125 ml)
Salt and white pepper to taste

Wash spinach under cold running water; do not dry. Place in a large frying pan, cover, and cook just until limp. Squeeze out any excess moisture and mince. Season spinach with salt and pepper and spoon into a buttered baking dish. Arrange fish fillets on top. Melt butter in a saucepan; blend in flour and cook and stir 2 minutes, not allowing flour to brown. Gradually stir in half-and-half and cook until thickened, stirring occasionally. Stir in wine and cheese. Season with salt and pepper. Spoon sauce over fish. Bake in a preheated 375°F (190°C) oven for 20 minutes or until flesh of fish separates when tested with a fork. Place under a broiler to brown the top.
Makes 4 servings

FISH SOUFFLÉ FLORENTINE

A charming restaurant in Lyon named Daniel and Denise makes a specialty of this glorious soufflé-topped fish entrée. It comes to the table high and billowy in a shiny copper pan.

2 shallots or green onions (white part only), chopped
3 tablespoons (45 ml) butter
1 large bunch spinach (about 1 pound or 500 g), chopped
3 tablespoons (45 ml) heavy cream
Salt, white pepper, and freshly grated nutmeg to taste
1 pound (500 g) sole or turbot fillets
Salt and white pepper
4 eggs, separated
1 teaspoon (5 ml) grated lemon peel
1/2 teaspoon (2 ml) dry mustard
1/2 cup (125 ml) sour cream
2 egg whites

In a large frying pan sauté shallots in 1 tablespoon (15 ml) of the butter until soft. Add spinach and cook just until wilted, about 1 minute. Mix in cream, salt, pepper, and nutmeg and turn into a buttered baking dish about 10 inches (25 cm) in diameter. Season fish fillets with salt and pepper and sauté in remaining butter, turning to brown both sides. Place fish, with pan juices, on top of spinach. Beat egg yolks with lemon peel and mustard until thick and pale in color. Mix in sour cream. Beat all 6 egg whites until stiff, glossy peaks form and fold into the egg yolk mixture. Spread over the fish. Bake in a preheated 375°F (190°C) oven for 20 minutes, or until puffed and golden brown.
Makes 4 servings

TROUT IN PARCHMENT

In a little family-run trattoria in Bellagio, Italy, one rainswept night, I sampled this glory, cooked in a steam-puffed paper casing. This recipe may be adapted to sole or other white-fleshed fish fillets or steaks.

3 shallots or green onions (white part only), minced
3 tablespoons (45 ml) butter
4 ounces (125 g) mushrooms, sliced or chopped
1 garlic clove, minced
2 tablespoons (30 ml) minced parsley
4 small trout
Salt and white pepper
1-1/2 teaspoons (7 ml) chopped fresh oregano, or
1/2 teaspoon (2 ml) crushed dried oregano
1 tablespoon (15 ml) each fresh lemon juice and olive oil
1 lemon, thinly sliced

In a frying pan slowly sauté shallots in butter until soft. Add mushrooms and sauté just until glazed. Remove from heat and stir in garlic and parsley. Wash trout and pat dry with paper towels; stuff each fish with sautéed vegetables and place on an oiled rectangle of parchment or aluminum foil large enough to encase fish completely. Sprinkle with salt, pepper, oregano, lemon juice, and oil. Arrange 1 or 2 lemon slices on top of each fish. Bring up parchment or foil and fold tightly with double folds at top and ends to seal. Place on a baking sheet and bake in a preheated 400°F (210°C) oven for 15 to 20 minutes, or until flesh of fish separates when tested with a fork.
Makes 4 servings

TROUT ORIENTAL STYLE

A toasty finish of browned sesame seeds enhances gingered and soy-glazed fish.

4 medium trout
1/3 cup (75 ml) rice wine or dry sherry
3 tablespoons (45 ml) soy sauce
2 tablespoons (30 ml) peanut or
    safflower oil
1-1/2 tablespoons (25 ml) fresh lime
    or lemon juice
2 teaspoons (10 ml) brown sugar
2 slices ginger root, slivered, or,
    1/4 teaspoon (1 ml) ground ginger
4 teaspoons (20 ml) sesame seeds

Place fish in a shallow pan. Mix together rice wine, soy, oil, lime juice, sugar, and ginger root; pour over fish, cover, and chill 1 to 2 hours. Toast sesame seeds by stirring in an ungreased frying pan over low heat for 3 to 4 minutes, or until light brown. Drain marinade and bake fish in a preheated 375°F (190°C) oven for 20 minutes or until flesh of fish separates when tested with a fork. (Fish may also be grilled or broiled.) Place on individual plates and sprinkle toasted seeds over fish.
Makes 4 servings

BAKED TROUT WITH CORIANDER MASALA

Pradeep Rao, a superb bachelor cook, enchants his dinner guests with exotically spiced dishes. His recipe for stuffed trout derives from his southern Indian heritage.

4 medium trout
1 teaspoon (5 ml) salt
Juice of 1/2 lemon
2 tablespoons (30 ml) safflower oil
4 tablespoons (60 ml) butter
1 teaspoon (5 ml) black mustard seeds
1/2 cup (125 ml) unsalted cashews,
    chopped
2 teaspoons (10 ml) grated ginger root
1 tablespoon (15 ml) minced garlic
1-1/2 cups (375 ml) minced onions
1/2 teaspoon (2 ml) ground turmeric
Masala, following
1/2 teaspoon (2 ml) freshly ground
    black pepper
4 large tomatoes, peeled, seeded, and
    chopped
1/2 cup (125 ml) unsweetened
    shredded coconut
2 tablespoons (30 ml) chopped fresh
    coriander

Wash trout under cold running water and pat dry with paper towels. Sprinkle with salt and rub with lemon juice; let stand 15 to 20 minutes. Meanwhile, spread oil over the bottom and sides of a shallow ovenproof serving dish. Melt butter in a frying pan; add mustard seeds and cashews and sauté for 5 minutes, stirring. Add ginger, garlic, and onions and cook until onions are translucent. Add turmeric, Masala, and pepper and mix well. Cook 5 minutes. Add tomatoes, coconut, and fresh coriander and cook 5 minutes longer. Stuff fish with vegetable-spice mixture. Place fish in greased baking pan, cover with aluminum foil and bake in a preheated 400°F (210°C) oven for 15 to 20 minutes, or until flesh of fish separates when tested with a fork.
Makes 4 entrée servings or
6 to 8 first-course servings

MASALA In a frying pan place 2 teaspoons (10 ml) coriander seeds, 1 whole clove, seeds from 2 cardamom pods, 1 very small dried red chili pepper, and 3/4 teaspoon (3 ml) cumin seeds. Cook over medium heat, stirring, until seeds toast lightly. Pour into a mortar or a spice grinder and grind to a fine powder.

Stocks & Sauces

COURT BOUILLON

Here is a basic stock for poaching a large whole salmon, lingcod, or other large fish.

8 cups (2 L) water
2 cups (500 ml) dry white wine or vermouth
1/2 cup (125 ml) white wine vinegar
1 to 2 large onions, sliced
2 carrots, cut in 1-inch (3 cm) chunks
1 celery stalk, cut in pieces
1 bay leaf
1-1/2 teaspoons (7 ml) chopped fresh thyme, or
    1/2 teaspoon (2 ml) crushed dried thyme
2 parsley sprigs
2 teaspoons (10 ml) salt
Few whole cloves and peppercorns

Combine all ingredients and bring to a boil. Simmer 1 hour before adding fish.
Makes about 10 cups (2.5 L)

RED WINE VARIATION Dry red wine may substitute for white wine for an aromatic broth especially suitable for salmon.

FISH STOCK

For a richer stock, suitable for poaching small chunks of fish to be used in a soup, fish bones and heads enrich the broth.

1 to 2 pounds (500 g to 1 kg) fish bones and heads*
6 cups (1.5 L) water
2 cups (500 ml) dry white wine or vermouth
1 tablespoon (15 ml) chopped fresh thyme, or
    1 teaspoon (5 ml) crushed dried thyme
2 onions, peeled and stuck with 2 whole cloves
2 carrots, diced
2 garlic cloves
1 bay leaf
Salt to taste
4 peppercorns

In a large pot simmer fish bones and heads in water for 30 minutes. Strain through a fine sieve. Return stock to pot and add remaining ingredients. Bring to a boil and simmer for 20 minutes before adding fish.
Makes about 7 cups (1.75 L)

*Save trimmings from fish and freeze for stock, or ask for trimmings from a fish store.

CLARIFIED FISH STOCK FOR ASPIC

Prepare stock as above and chill. Lift off any fat that has congealed on top. Beat 4 egg whites in a large mixing bowl with 2 cups (500 ml) of the cold stock. Bring remaining stock to a boil in a saucepan. Then, beating the egg white mixture with a whisk, pour in about 1 cup (250 ml) of the hot stock in a very thin stream. Pour the mixture back into the saucepan and place over medium heat. Heat, beating with a whisk, until a simmer is reached. Turn off heat and let stand 15 minutes. Line a colander with several thicknesses of cheesecloth and place it over a bowl. Gently ladle the stock and egg whites into the cheesecloth, letting the clarified stock drain through. If desired, the stock may be boiled down further until reduced to a gelatinous consistency.

CUCUMBER SAUCE

A refreshingly cool sauce to serve with cold poached salmon or halibut.

1 small cucumber, peeled, halved, and seeded
Salt
1 cup (250 ml) sour cream, or
   2/3 cup (150 ml) sour cream mixed with
   1/3 cup (75 ml) yogurt
1 teaspoon (5 ml) chopped fresh dill weed, or
   1/4 teaspoon (1 ml) crushed dried dill weed
1/4 teaspoon (1 ml) each salt and sugar
Pinch white pepper
1 teaspoon (5 ml) white wine vinegar
2 tablespoons (30 ml) chopped parsley

Cut cucumber into 1/4-inch (6 mm) dice and place in a strainer. Sprinkle with salt, toss, and let stand for 20 minutes for moisture to exude. Mix together sour cream, dill weed, salt, sugar, pepper, and wine vinegar. Mix in cucumbers and parsley. Cover and chill.
Makes 2 cups (500 ml)

CRÈME FRAÎCHE

Crème fraîche is an excellent substitute for sour cream. This is a close approximation of the French product. It is easily made and will keep about four weeks under refrigeration.

2 cups (500 ml) heavy cream
1 cup (250 ml) sour cream

Combine heavy cream and sour cream in a saucepan. Heat, stirring, until just tepid, about 80° to 85°F (30°C). Pour into a jar, cover, and let stand at room temperature overnight, then chill thoroughly.
Makes about 3 cups (250 ml)

SOUR CREAM-SHALLOT SAUCE

A versatile sauce to spoon over broiled or barbecued fish or a seafood salad. To reduce calories, substitute yogurt for one-third to one-half of the sour cream.

1 cup (250 ml) sour cream
2 shallots or green onions (white part only), minced
3 tablespoons (45 ml) chopped parsley
Salt and white pepper to taste
Dash Tabasco sauce

Mix all ingredients together. Cover and chill.
Makes 1 cup (250 ml)

GUACAMOLE

Mashed and seasoned avocado makes a buttery, smooth sauce to accompany baked or broiled white fish fillets. It is also a spectacular coating for a baked and skinned whole salmon, served cold at a summer brunch or garden party. The flavor of avocados varies throughout the year; add extra seasoning and lemon juice if necessary.

2 large avocados, peeled and halved
1/4 cup (50 ml) fresh lemon or lime juice or to taste
1/2 teaspoon (2 ml) salt
1 garlic clove, minced
1 green onion, chopped
Freshly ground black pepper to taste
Dash Tabasco sauce
1/4 cup (50 ml) minced fresh coriander (optional)

Set aside 1 of the avocado seeds. Mash avocados with a fork and mix in lemon juice, salt, garlic, onion, pepper, Tabasco, and fresh coriander. Cover and chill with a seed buried in the sauce to retard discoloration.
Makes about 1-1/2 cups (375 ml)

SPRIGHTLY CHILI DIP

This is an excellent sauce for shrimp, crab, or a selection of iced shellfish.

3/4 cup (175 ml) catsup
1/2 cup (125 ml) chili sauce
2 tablespoons (30 ml) fresh lemon juice
1 tablespoon (15 ml) each prepared horseradish and grated onion
1/2 teaspoon (2 ml) Worcestershire sauce
1/4 teaspoon (1 ml) dry mustard
Few drops Tabasco sauce

Mix all ingredients together. Cover and chill.
Makes about 1-1/2 cups (375 ml)

AVOCADO SAUCE

The avocado has a natural affinity for seafood. Use this pretty sauce as a dip for crab legs or shrimp.

1 large avocado, peeled and halved
1 tablespoon (15 ml) fresh lemon juice
1 teaspoon (5 ml) Worcestershire sauce
1/4 teaspoon (1 ml) salt
1 garlic clove, minced
3 ounces (75 g) cream cheese, at room temperature
1/4 cup (50 ml) sour cream
2 tablespoons (30 ml) minced green onion or chives

Place avocado in a blender or a food processor fitted with a steel blade and add lemon juice, Worcestershire, salt, and garlic. Blend until smooth. Add cream cheese and sour cream, blending until smooth. Remover from blender and mix in onion. Place in a container, cover, and chill.
Makes about 1-1/4 cups (300 ml)

SALSA VERDE

A bright green Italian sauce for cold poached halibut, lingcod, or sea bass.

3/4 cup (175 ml) minced parsley
2 green onions, chopped
2 tablespoons (30 ml) chopped capers
3 garlic cloves, minced
1/4 cup (50 ml) olive oil
2 tablespoons (30 ml) white wine vinegar
Salt and freshly ground black pepper to taste

Mix all ingredients together. Cover and chill.
Makes about 1 cup (250 ml)

TOMATILLO SAUCE

The unique flavor of the tomatillo, or Mexican husk tomato, is the basis of this cooked green sauce that goes well with mild-flavored fish.

1 medium onion, chopped
1 tablespoon (15 ml) corn or safflower
    oil
1 pound (500 g) fresh tomatillos,
    husked, or
    16 ounces (450 g) canned toma-
    tillos, drained
1 tablespoon (15 ml) chopped canned
    peeled green chili
2 tablespoons (30 ml) minced fresh
    coriander
Salt and freshly ground black pepper
    to taste

In a frying pan, cook onion in oil until translucent; set aside. If using fresh tomatillos, cook in boiling salted water to cover until tender, about 10 minutes; drain. Purée tomatillos in a blender with just enough water to make a smooth sauce; add to onions. Add chili and fresh coriander and cook, stirring occasionally, until slightly thickened. Season to taste with salt and pepper.
Makes about 2 cups (500 ml)

SAUCE PROVENÇALE

Sun-ripened tomatoes are best for this robust cooked French sauce. Especially good on sautéed or grilled fish steaks.

1/2 cup (125 ml) olive oil
8 ripe medium tomatoes (about 3
    pounds or 1.5 kg), peeled, seeded,
    and chopped
1 teaspoon (5 ml) each salt and sugar
1/2 teaspoon (2 ml) freshly ground
    black pepper
3 garlic cloves, minced
2 tablespoons (30 ml) chopped parsley

Heat oil in a heavy pan and add tomatoes, salt, sugar, pepper, garlic, and parsley. Cover and simmer 30 to 40 minutes or until the sauce is smooth and thickened.
Makes about 2 cups (500 ml)

NANTUA SAUCE

A luxurious sauce to glorify mild-flavored fish.

4 tablespoons (60 ml) butter, melted
4 ounces (125 g) cooked small shrimp
2 tablespoons (30 ml) each butter and
    flour
1/4 teaspoon (1 ml) salt
Dash white pepper
1/4 cup (50 ml) each chicken broth,
    clam juice, and
    dry white wine or vermouth
1/2 cup (125 ml) half-and-half
1/2 teaspoon (2 ml) fresh lemon juice

Combine melted butter and shrimp in a blender and purée until smooth; set aside. Melt the 2 tablespoons (30 ml) butter in a saucepan and blend in flour, salt, and pepper; cook and stir 2 minutes, not allowing flour to brown. Stir in chicken broth, clam juice, and wine and cook, stirring constantly, until thickened. Reduce heat and stir in half-and-half. Cook over low heat, stirring constantly, until mixture thickens and bubbles. Remove from heat and stir in lemon juice and shrimp-butter mixture.
Makes about 1-1/2 cups (375 ml)

MAYONNAISE

Homemade mayonnaise is a classic accompaniment to fish. It is wonderfully simple to make and is far superior to the commercial product.

1 whole egg or 2 egg yolks
1 tablespoon (15 ml) vinegar or fresh
   lemon juice
1 teaspoon (5 ml) salt
1/2 teaspoon (2 ml) dry mustard
Freshly ground black pepper
1 cup (250 ml) safflower oil

CLASSIC WHISK METHOD Place eggs or egg yolks in a bowl and beat for 1 minute with a wire whisk. Add vinegar, salt, mustard, and pepper and beat 30 seconds longer. Gradually pour in oil, drop by drop, beating until thickened. Turn into a container, cover, and chill.

BLENDER OR FOOD PROCESSOR METHOD Place in a blender or a food processor fitted with a steel blade the egg or egg yolks, vinegar, salt, mustard, and pepper. Blend a few seconds. Gradually pour in oil in a slow steady stream, blending until smooth and thickened. Turn into a container, cover, and chill.

Makes about 1 cup (250 ml)

GREEN MAYONNAISE

A beautiful green sauce for cold fish or shellfish.

8 large spinach leaves
4 parsley sprigs
2 green onions, coarsely sliced
1 teaspoon (5 ml) chopped fresh
   tarragon, or
   1/4 teaspoon (1 ml) crushed dried
   tarragon
1/2 teaspoon (2 ml) each salt and dry
   mustard
Dash white pepper
1 egg
3 tablespoons (45 ml) white wine
   vinegar
1 cup (250 ml) safflower oil

Place in a blender or a food processor fitted with a steel blade the spinach, parsley, onions, tarragon, salt, mustard, pepper, egg, and half of the vinegar. Blend a few seconds. Slowly pour in oil, blending until thickened. Mix in remaining vinegar. Turn into a container, cover, and chill.
Makes about 1 cup (250 ml)

PESTO MAYONNAISE

Fresh basil and garlic produce a robust Genoese sauce for poached, baked, or fried fish. Make Pesto Sauce in quantity in late summer at the peak of the basil season; it freezes well for year-round pleasure.

Pesto Sauce, following
2 egg yolks
1-1/2 tablespoons (25 ml) each lemon
   juice and white wine vinegar
1/2 teaspoon (2 ml) each salt, sugar,
   and dry mustard
Dash white pepper
7/8 cup (200 ml) safflower oil

Prepare Pesto Sauce and set aside. Place in a blender or a food processor fitted with a steel blade the egg yolks, lemon juice, vinegar, salt, sugar, mustard, and pepper. Blend a few seconds and, with motor running, gradually pour in oil. Blend in Pesto Sauce, turn into a container, cover, and chill.
Makes about 1-1/2 cups (375 ml)

PESTO SAUCE Place in a blender or a food processor fitted with a steel blade 2 tablespoons (30 ml) olive oil, 1/2 cup (125 ml) packed basil leaves, 1 garlic clove, 1-1/2 tablespoons (25 ml) pine nuts, and 2 tablespoons (30 ml) grated Parmesan cheese. Blend until smooth. Turn into a container, cover, and chill (or freeze if you are making it to keep). To prevent discoloration, pour a thin film of olive oil on top before sealing the container. Makes about 1/2 cup (125 ml).

TAPENADE

Serve this zestful Provençal sauce with any cold poached fish or shellfish.

1 egg or 2 egg yolks
1-1/2 tablespoons (25 ml) each fresh
    lemon juice and white wine vinegar
1 teaspoon (5 ml) each salt, sugar,
    and dry mustard
1 cup (250 ml) safflower oil
3 tablespoons (45 ml) chopped capers
1 garlic clove, minced
4 anchovy fillets, chopped
3 tablespoons (45 ml) chopped parsley
1/2 teaspoon (2 ml) grated lemon peel

Place in a blender or a food processor fitted with a steel blade the egg, lemon juice, vinegar, salt, sugar, and mustard. Blend for a few seconds. With motor running, gradually pour in oil in a slow, steady stream and blend until smooth. Stir in capers, garlic, anchovies, parsley, and lemon peel. Turn into a container, cover, and chill.
Makes about 1-1/2 cups (375 ml)

PISTACHIO MAYONNAISE

Green pistachios and herbs give a homemade mayonnaise an appealing color and flavor. Superlative with barbecued or poached salmon or halibut steaks.

2 egg yolks
1-1/2 tablespoons (25 ml) each fresh
    lemon juice and white wine vinegar
1 teaspoon (5 ml) each salt
    and dry mustard
7/8 cup (200 ml) safflower oil
1 garlic clove, chopped
1/3 cup (75 ml) chopped spinach
    leaves
2 tablespoons (30 ml) chopped parsley
1-1/2 teaspoons (7 ml) chopped fresh
    tarragon, or
    1/2 teaspoon (2 ml) crushed dried
    tarragon
1/4 cup (50 ml) unsalted pistachio
    nuts

Place in a blender or a food processor fitted with a steel blade the egg yolks, lemon juice, vinegar, salt, and mustard. With motor running, gradually pour in oil, blending to a smooth sauce. Add garlic, spinach, parsley, tarragon, and nuts and blend 5 seconds longer or until sauce is flecked green. Turn into a container, cover, and chill.
Makes about 1-1/2 cups (375 ml)

GREEN GODDESS SAUCE

Green Goddess Sauce originated in San Francisco. It is superb with cold crab, lobster, or shrimp salad.

3/4 cup (175 ml) Mayonnaise, page 119
2 tablespoons (30 ml) tarragon-
    flavored white wine vinegar
1 garlic clove, minced
1-1/2 teaspoons (7 ml) chopped fresh
    tarragon, or
    1/2 teaspoon (2 ml) crushed dried
    tarragon
3 anchovy fillets, minced
1/3 cup (75 ml) packed minced parsley
1/3 cup (75 ml) sour cream
Freshly ground black pepper

Place in a blender or a food processor fitted with a steel blade the Mayonnaise, vinegar, garlic, tarragon, anchovy fillets, and parsley. Blend until parsley is very finely puréed. Add sour cream and blend just until incorporated. Turn into a container, cover, and chill.
Makes about 1-1/4 cups (300 ml)

SAUCE GRIBICHE

Herb- and egg-enriched mayonnaise is an excellent sauce for cold poached fish or a fish salad.

2 egg yolks or 1 egg
Salt and freshly ground black pepper
1 teaspoon (5 ml) Dijon-style mustard
3 tablespoons (45 ml) white wine vinegar
1/2 cup (125 ml) each olive oil and safflower oil
2 shallots or green onions (white part only), minced
1/4 cup (50 ml) chopped parsley
1-1/2 teaspoons (7 ml) minced fresh tarragon, or
    1/2 teaspoon (2 ml) crushed dried tarragon
1 hard-cooked egg, sieved or chopped

Place egg yolks in a bowl and beat in salt, pepper, mustard, and vinegar. Gradually add oils in a slow steady stream, beating until thick. (Or if desired, make in a blender or a food processor, as for mayonnaise, see page 119.) Stir in shallots, parsley, tarragon, and egg. Cover and chill.
Makes about 1-3/4 cups (425 ml)

SAUCE REMOULADE

This is an excellent sauce for any cold poached fish or shellfish.

1 cup (250 ml) Mayonnaise, page 119
1 garlic clove, minced
1-1/2 teaspoons (7 ml) minced fresh tarragon, or
    1/2 teaspoon (2 ml) crushed dried tarragon
1/2 teaspoon (2 ml) dry mustard
1 hard-cooked egg, minced
2 teaspoons (10 ml) capers, chopped
1 tablespoon (15 ml) chopped parsley
1/2 teaspoon (2 ml) anchovy paste

Mix all ingredients together. Cover and chill at least 1 hour before serving.
Makes about 1-1/4 cups (300 ml)

THOUSAND ISLAND DRESSING

A favorite sauce for a crab, shrimp, or turbot or snapper salad.

1 cup (250 ml) Mayonnaise, page 119
1 green onion, minced
1 hard-cooked egg, minced
1/4 cup (50 ml) chili sauce
1/2 teaspoon (2 ml) dry mustard
2 tablespoons (30 ml) minced parsley
Few drops fresh lemon juice

Mix all ingredients together. Cover and chill at least 1 hour before serving.
Makes about 1-1/2 cups (375 ml)

AIOLI

Garlicky mayonnaise makes an excellent dip for cold cooked shrimp or hot-broiled, baked, or poached fish. In France it is the traditional accompaniment to salt cod.

1 egg
2 tablespoons (30 ml) white wine vinegar
1 tablespoon (15 ml) fresh lemon juice
1 teaspoon (5 ml) each salt and Dijon-style mustard
4 or 5 garlic cloves
1 cup (250 ml) safflower oil

Place in a blender container or a food processor fitted with a steel blade the egg, vinegar, lemon juice, salt, mustard, and garlic and blend until smooth. With motor running, gradually pour in oil in a fine, steady stream, blending to make a thick mayonnaise. Turn into a container, cover, and chill.
Makes about 1-1/4 cups (300 ml)

SKORDALIA

Greek garlic mayonnaise is punctuated with toasted almonds or pine nuts for a delicious accompaniment to baked halibut, poached salmon, or cold cooked shrimp. This sauce is a variation of the more common mashed potato version of *skordalia*.

1/3 cup (75 ml) pine nuts or almonds
1 egg
1-1/2 tablespoons (25 ml) each fresh lemon juice and white wine vinegar
3/4 teaspoon (4 ml) salt
3 garlic cloves, minced
1/2 cup (125 ml) each olive oil and safflower oil

Lightly toast the nuts by spreading them in a shallow baking pan and placing them in a preheated 325°F (160°C) oven for 8 to 10 minutes. Place in a blender or a food processor fitted with a steel blade the egg, lemon juice, vinegar, salt, and garlic and blend a few seconds. With the motor running, slowly pour in the olive and safflower oils. Add nuts and blend a few seconds. Turn into a container, cover, and chill.
Makes about 1-1/2 cups (375 ml)

BROWNED BUTTER

When heated to a toasty brown, butter develops a marvelous nutty flavor that is superb with fish.

Heat unsalted butter slowly in a small frying pan or long-handled copper serving dish until it melts, bubbles, and turns a light golden brown. Remove from heat immediately to avoid further browning.

LEMON BUTTER PATTIES

Flavored butter is super-convenient to have on hand as an instant sauce to melt into baked salmon or grilled trout.

1/4 pound (125 g) butter
1 teaspoon (5 ml) grated lemon peel
2 tablespoons (30 ml) minced chives or green onions
1/2 teaspoon (2 ml) chopped fresh tarragon (optional)
Salt and white pepper to taste

In a small bowl combine butter, lemon peel, chives, and tarragon, mixing until blended. Season with salt and pepper. Shape into a roll on waxed paper, roll up, and chill. Slice into patties.
Makes about 8 patties

MUSTARD BUTTER SAUCE

A piquant mustard sauce is excellent on poached or broiled white-fleshed fish. French mustard is essential.

2 tablespoons (30 ml) chopped shallots or green onions (white part only)
2 tablespoons (30 ml) red wine vinegar
1 tablespoon (15 ml) cold water
1/4 pound (125 g) butter
1 tablespoon (15 ml) Dijon-style mustard
3 tablespoons (45 ml) minced parsley, or
1 tablespoon (15 ml) chopped chives
Salt and white pepper to taste

In a small saucepan combine shallots and vinegar. Bring to a boil and cook until almost all the liquid has evaporated. Remove from heat, let cool briefly, and add cold water. Add half of the butter, about 2 tablespoons (30 ml) at a time, beating vigorously with a wire whisk. Return to low heat and continue adding butter without letting the sauce come to a boil. When creamy, smooth, and slightly thickened, add mustard and parsley. Season with salt and pepper.
Makes about 2/3 cup (150 ml)

BEURRE BLANC

This French invention is one of the simplest, yet most exquisite of sauces for fish. Wait until the last minute to make it, as it will not hold. Serve over poached or broiled fillets of sole or turbot or baked fish.

2 tablespoons (30 ml) minced shallots
   or green onions (white part only)
1/4 cup (50 ml) dry white wine or
   vermouth
1/4 cup (50 ml) white wine vinegar
1/4 pound (125 g) unsalted butter
Salt and white pepper to taste

Place the shallots, wine, and vinegar in a saucepan and cook until reduced to 2 tablespoons (30 ml). Add butter, 1 tablespoon (15 ml) at a time, beating constantly with a wire whisk over low heat until sauce is thick and creamy. Season with salt and pepper. Serve immediately.
Makes about 1/2 cup (125 ml).

GARLIC BEURRE BLANC Reduce amount of shallots to 1 tablespoon (15 ml) and add 2 minced garlic cloves to the wine and vinegar. Reduce as above. Whisk in 4 tablespoons (60 ml) butter, 1 tablespoon (15 ml) at a time, then beat in 3 tablespoons (45 ml) Crème Fraîche, page 116, or heavy cream; cook until reduced slightly. Season to taste with salt and white pepper.

HOLLANDAISE SAUCE

The classic hollandaise may be made in various ways: with a wire whisk, a blender, or a food processor. If the sauce should separate, emulsify it again by beating in a little boiling water. Unsalted butter gives a superior product.

1/4 pound (125 g) unsalted butter
3 egg yolks
1-1/2 tablespoons (25 ml) fresh lemon
   juice
1/4 teaspoon (1 ml) salt
Dash white pepper
1/2 teaspoon (2 ml) grated lemon peel
   or Dijon-style mustard

CLASSIC WHISK METHOD Melt butter until bubbly and keep warm. Beat egg yolks with a wire whisk in the top of a double boiler until pale lemon in color, about 1 minute. Beat in lemon juice, salt, pepper, and lemon peel. Place yolk mixture over simmering water and gently beat in butter in a slow, steady stream, omitting milky residue at the bottom of butter pan. Beat until thickened. Turn into a sauce bowl and keep warm in a pan of tepid water if not using immediately.

BLENDER METHOD Melt butter until bubbly and keep warm. Rinse out the blender container with very hot water and drain. Put in the blender container egg yolks, lemon juice, salt, pepper, and lemon peel and blend for a few seconds. With motor running, gradually pour in butter in a slow steady stream, omitting the milky residue at the bottom of the butter pan, and blend just until smooth. Turn sauce into the top of a double boiler or small saucepan and heat gently.

FOOD PROCESSOR METHOD Melt butter until bubbly and keep warm. In a food processor fitted with a steel blade, place egg yolks, lemon juice, salt, pepper, and lemon peel. Process for 3 seconds and, still processing, pour in melted butter. Turn into a sauce bowl and keep warm in a pan of tepid water if not using immediately.

Makes about 1 cup (250 ml)

MOUSSELINE SAUCE Prepare Hollandaise Sauce, above. Whip 1/2 cup (125 ml) heavy cream until stiff and fold in. Makes about 2 cups (500 ml).

BEARNAISE SAUCE

A classic sauce that does wonders for a variety of fish.

3 tablespoons (45 ml) white wine vinegar
1-1/2 teaspoons (7 ml) minced fresh tarragon, or
   1/2 teaspoon (2 ml) crushed dried tarragon
1 parsley sprig
2 teaspoons (10 ml) chopped shallots or green onions (white part only)
3 egg yolks
1/2 teaspoon (2 ml) Dijon-style mustard
3/4 cup (175 ml) butter

Place in a saucepan vinegar, tarragon, parsley, and shallots and cook over medium heat until reduced to about 1-1/2 tablespoons (25 ml); strain and set aside. Beat egg yolks in the top of a double boiler with a wire whisk until pale lemon in color, about 1 minute. Beat in the strained vinegar mixture and mustard and beat a few seconds. Melt butter until bubbly. Place yolk mixture over simmering water and gently beat in melted butter in a slow steady stream, omitting milky residue at the bottom of butter pan and beating until thickened. Turn into a sauce bowl and keep warm in a pan of tepid water if not using immediately.
Makes about 1 cup (250 ml)

CAPERED HOLLANDAISE

This zestful sauce will enhance barbecued salmon or baked halibut.

1 tablespoon (15 ml) capers
2 shallots or green onions (white part only), chopped
2 tablespoons (30 ml) butter
2 tablespoons (30 ml) dry white wine or vermouth
Hollandaise Sauce, page 124
1/2 teaspoon (2 ml) Dijon-style mustard
1/4 teaspoon (1 ml) Worcestershire sauce

In a small saucepan sauté capers and shallots in butter until glazed. Add wine and simmer 1 minute. Remove from heat and stir in remaining ingredients. Turn into a sauce bowl and keep warm in a pan of tepid water if not using immediately.
Makes about 1 cup (250 ml)

A Guide to Fish & Shellfish

A bewildering variety of fish and shellfish inhabit the world today—it is estimated that there are 30,000 species of finned fish alone, more than any other class of vertebrates. These fish and shellfish show a great diversity of structure, size, and color, and are found in bodies of water from mountain torrents to the depths of the oceans. This guide consists of those species most commonly available in the United States.

ABALONE There are eight species of this univalve saltwater mollusk on the Pacific Coast, including green, northern green, red, white, pink, black, threaded, and Japanese or pinto abalones. They are available commercially year-round in the coastal states, and are shipped frozen from Mexico. As a sport fish, their garnering is limited by law to specific seasons. The meat of the abalone may be tough if not cooked properly; it should be sliced into thin steaks, pounded to tenderize, and sautéed quickly. Abalone are being seeded and raised to a 2-inch size at a California natural harbor at Port Hueneme. They are currently marketed mainly to upscale restaurants.

AHI See Tuna.

ALBACORE See Tuna.

ALEWIFE See Herring.

AMBERJACK See Jack.

BASS A confusing category, as many fish given this name, including black basses and white seabasses, do not belong to the bass family. The two main divisions of the bass family are the sea basses and the striped basses. See Sea Bass and Striped Bass.

BLACKBACK See Winter Flounder under Flounder.

BLACK BASS These fresh-water fish are not true basses, but are members of the sunfish family. They are popular sport fish with a lean, fine-textured flesh and are not available commercially. The two best-known black bass are the largemouth bass, which is widely distributed across the United States and varies greatly in size, and the smallmouth bass, also found in many parts of the country and averaging 2 pounds. Two other black bass that are good table fish are the redeye bass, found in the South, and the spotted bass, found in the South and the Midwest.

BLACK COD See Sablefish.

BLACKFISH See Sea Bass.

BLUEFISH A saltwater fish of the Atlantic Coast, baby bluefish are sometimes called "snappers" because of their sharp teeth; adult bluefish are sometimes called "choppers." The bluefish is a migrating fish, available fresh in winter and early spring in the South, and in late spring, summer, and fall in the North. It ranges in size from less than 1 pound to over 20 pounds. Small bluefish have a mild-flavored flesh; larger fish have a fuller flavor. Bluefish have a high fat content and may be baked or charcoal broiled.

BLUEGILL See Sunfish.

BOCACCIO See Rockfish.

BONITA See Tuna.

BREAM See Sunfish.

BUFFALOFISH See Sucker.

BULLHEAD See Catfish.

BURBOT See Cod.

BUTTERFISH A silvery saltwater fish found off the Atlantic and Gulf coasts in summer and late fall. Butterfish average in size from 1/4 to 1-1/4 pounds and have a soft, oily flesh.

CANDLEFISH See Smelt.

CARP A fresh-water fish found in streams and lakes throughout the United States; one of the domesticated species is the Chinese golden carp. It has been farmed for centuries. The carp has a firm, mild-flavored flesh that is low to moderate in fat content and may be cooked by almost any method; it is usually sold in sizes ranging from 2 to 8 pounds.

CATFISH The catfish is the basis of a large commercial farming industry as well as being a popular sport fish, and thus it is usually available fresh in most of the United States. It is a versatile fish with a lean, mild-flavored tender flesh and may be cooked by almost any method. The most commonly available species are the blue catfish and the channel catfish; there are also the bullheads, and the flathead, gafftopsail, and white catfishes. The size may range from 1 to 40 pounds.

CAVIAR The roe or eggs of certain fish, processed with salt to flavor and preserve them naturally. Available in both affordable and luxury styles, caviar comes from sturgeon, salmon, and golden whitefish; colors range from golden to red, to shades of black. Fresh caviar must be kept refrigerated and should be used promptly after purchase; Malassol, the premium grade, is the least salty and the most perishable. Vacuum-packed, pasteurized caviar does not require refrigeration, but should be stored in a cool, dark place and used within three months. Once the jar is opened, refrigerate and use within a day or two. Following are some types of caviar available in North America.

Lumpfish Caviar from Arctic waters, the least expensive variety, comes in black, red, and golden hues. The small eggs have a pronounced flavor that is good in dips and hors d'oeuvres.

Whitefish Caviar from the Northern Great Lakes is a small firm-textured egg with a delicate crunch. The black is used like lumpfish, but the golden is milder, good for a garnish, salads, or pasta.

Salmon Caviar from the Pacific Northwest has large, translucent grains in two natural colors: "red" is actually deep coral from silver salmon; "natural" is from chum salmon and a bit paler. Flavorful and colorful, salmon roe is good in omelets, canapés, and toppings.

American Sturgeon Caviar from the Mississippi River and its tributaries is medium grained, pearly gray-black. Mild and tangy, it is classically served on ice with toast and lemon wedges.

Imported Sturgeon Caviars from the Caspian Sea and Volga River have a mild, memorable, nonfishy flavor. Traditionally they are served iced with toast. Beluga is large grained, pearl gray to black. Osetra is medium grained with gold highlights. Sevruga is small grained with deep gray tones. Pressed has some intact grains but a somewhat "jammy" consistency.

CHANNEL BASS See Red Drum under Drum.

CHAR See Trout.

CHUB See Cisco under Whitefish.

CISCO See Whitefish.

CLAM A bivalve mollusk found on both coasts. Atlantic Coast clams include the softshell and the hardshell, or quahog. Small hardshell clams are called "Little Necks" (not the same as the littleneck clams of the Pacific Coast), and medium-sized hardshells are called "Cherrystones." Also on the Atlantic Coast are razor and bar clams (the latter are also called skimmer or surf clams). The Pacific Coast also has softshell clams. Hard-shelled clams include razors, littlenecks, butter clams and horse clams. The Pismo and the geoduck are large hard-shelled clams. Clams are available commercially year-round but their gathering is regulated to certain seasons. Clams can be toxic due to pollution or certain feeding conditions; check with your state fishing authority before gathering them. Thirty small hard-shelled clams in the shell equal approximately 1 quart (1 L) of shucked clams; two 7-ounce (196 g) cans of minced clams may be substituted for approximately 3 pounds (1.5 kg) of small hard-shelled clams in many recipes.

COD The basic food fish throughout history, the cod is found in both the Atlantic and the Pacific oceans; there is one fresh-water species, the burbot. There are four main species of cod, all of them low in fat and mild in flavor, with tender flesh:

Atlantic Cod The most important of the cods commercially, the Atlantic cod varies greatly in size and is closely related to the Pacific cod.

Haddock Found on the Atlantic Coast, the haddock ranges in size from 1-1/2 to 7 pounds.

Hake An Atlantic fish, usually sold at 1 to 2 pounds. The silver hake is often marketed as whiting.

Pollock An Atlantic fish, usually sold at 4 to 5 pounds.

CORVINA See Weakfish under Drum.

CRAB Several species of these crustaceans are found on the American coasts:

Blue Crab An Atlantic Coast crab that appears inshore in warm weather. When the blue crab has shed its shell, it is known as a soft-shell crab and is usually 2 to 5 ounces in size; at this stage most of the crab is edible. Hard-shell blue crabs range from 4 to 16 ounces.

Dungeness Crab A Pacific Coast crab ranging from 1-3/4 to 4 pounds. It is available fresh November through June.

King Crab A northern Pacific crab called variously Alaska King, Japanese crab, and Russian crab, it averages 10 pounds in weight. The peak season for this crab is midwinter.

Red Crab An Atlantic Coast crab, averaging 1-1/4 to 2-1/4 pounds, it is often substituted for the King crab.

Other species include the snow crab, the rock crab, and the stone crab.

CRAPPIE See Sunfish.

CRAYFISH A fresh-water crustacean found across the United States but most plentiful in the South and the Northwest. There are many different species. Their gathering is regulated by state law. Crayfish may be poached and substituted for shrimp in many recipes.

CROAKER See Drum.

CUSK This is the same fish as scrod. A relative of the cod family, it is also known as tusk or moonfish. Although found on both sides of the North Atlantic year-round, cusk is most abundant in summer. It weighs from 2 to 15 pounds and is available fresh or frozen, usually as a fillet. It is suited for baking or grilling.

DOLPHIN Also called dolfinfish to distinguish it from the mammal dolphin, to which it is not related, the dolphin is a tropical and subtropical game fish known in Hawaii as mahi-mahi. It ranges in size from 2 to 50 pounds and can be cooked by almost any method. It is found on both coasts.

DRUM So-called because they actually do make a drumming sound, the drums include croakers and weakfish. Drums are found off both coasts, and the size of the species ranges from small to very large. They are generally low in fat content, with a mild-flavored flesh.

Atlantic Croaker The most common of the croakers, so-called because the drumming sound is more like a croak. This fish is found off the Atlantic Coast from New Jersey to Texas. It is usually sold at 1/2 to 3 pounds and is sometimes called "golden croaker." It is becoming increasingly popular as a market fish.

Freshwater Drum The only freshwater drum, sometimes called "white perch" or "sheepshead" and averaging 1-1/2 to 5 pounds. It is found in large rivers and lakes in the central United States.

Red Drum Sometimes called "channel bass" or "redfish," the red drum is found off the Atlantic and Gulf coasts in sizes ranging from 4 to over 20 pounds.

Weakfish A fine table fish with a white flesh, its name may derive from its delicate mouth structure. The weakfish is an Atlantic Coast fish; the spotted seatrout of the southern Atlantic and Gulf coasts and the white seabass and the corvina of the Pacific Coast are very closely related to it. The roe of the weakfish is considered a delicacy.

White Seabass A Pacific Coast fish, usually 15 to 20 pounds in weight. A fine food fish found in California markets in summer and fall.

Other drums that are good as table fish include the totuava and the spotfish croaker.

EEL Both American and European eels are born in the Sargasso Sea of the

North Atlantic; the American species of larvae then swim to the eastern Atlantic Coast, while the European species swim to the coast of Europe. The eels arrive on their respective coasts as elvers, or young eels, in the spring. Male eels remain in the tidal marshes and estuaries, while the females make their way up the rivers; when they have matured, the female eels rejoin the males, and they return to the Sargasso Sea to spawn. Eels are seasonal in late autumn and winter when they have matured and have turned black in color; at this time they may range in size from 1 to 5 pounds. Eels have a mild-flavored white flesh and may be cooked in a variety of ways. Fresh and smoked eel is considered a delicacy in Europe.

EULACHON See Smelt.

FLOUNDER A family of flat fish, some having both eyes on the left side. The flounder family includes the plaice, the halibut, the turbot, and several fish that are called "sole." In general flounders have a mild-flavored, tender white flesh.
American Plaice A northern Atlantic fish usually marketed at 2 to 3 pounds.
Halibut Fish given the name of halibut include the Atlantic halibut, the largest of the flounders, which is found in the northern Atlantic, and its counterpart, the Pacific halibut. There is also a California halibut and a Greenland halibut (the latter found on both coasts; see Turbot, following).
Pacific Sanddab A small Pacific Coast flounder; a fine food fish.
Sole The true Dover or English sole is not found in North American waters, but there are two Pacific Coast flounders marketed as "Dover sole" and "English sole" respectively; the starry flounder of the Pacific is also sometimes marketed as "sole." The larger summer flounder is known as "lemon sole," and the Pacific Coast has the petrale, butter, sand and Rex soles. The petrale is a large flounder of fine table quality, and the other three are small flounders that compare to it in quality.
Summer Flounder A northern Atlantic fish, sometimes called "fluke," it is most abundant in the summer and averages 3 to 5 pounds.
Turbot Like the true sole, the true turbot is a European fish not found in this country, though some Pacific flounders are given the name of turbot. On the Pacific Coast, the arrowtooth flounder is often sold as turbot. The Greenland halibut, found in both the Atlantic and the Pacific, is sometimes marketed as "Greenland turbot." Hake, whiting, and various flounders can be substituted for turbot.
Winter Flounder The winter flounder, also a northern Atlantic fish, is known as "lemon sole" when it weighs over 3 pounds, and as flounder or "blackback" under 3 pounds.

FLUKE See Summer Flounder under Flounder.

GAG See Grouper.

GOGGLE-EYE See Sunfish.

GREENLING A Pacific Coast fish. Small greenlings are sport fish, but the large (70 pounds or more) lingcod is a popular commercial fish that is low in fat content, with a delicately flavored, tender flesh.

GROUPER A saltwater fish found off both coasts, the grouper ranges from temperate to tropical waters and has a lean white flesh. The roe of some groupers, such as the gag, may be toxic. Species include the jewfish (the largest category of groupers and very good table fish); the red, rock, and speckled hinds; and the red, warsaw, and yellowmouth groupers.

GRUNT An inshore tropical and semitropical saltwater fish, its name is taken from the sound the fish makes when taken from the water. The porkfish of Florida is one of the best of the species; the pigfish and the white grunt are found off the Atlantic Coast. The grunt generally has a tender, white flesh.

HADDOCK See Cod.

HAKE See Cod.

HALIBUT See Flounder.

HERRING One of the most important commercial fishes throughout history, the herring is a silver-colored migratory fish that is high in protein. The two main species are the Atlantic herring and the Pacific herring. The alewife and the blueback herring are called "spring herring" and "summer herring" respectively because they leave the ocean and ascend fresh-water rivers to spawn. Different species spawn at different times, therefore there is no one season for fresh herring; most herring are salted or pickled. See also Sardine and Shad.

HIND See Grouper.

JACK A saltwater fish, found mostly in tropical and subtropical waters. This fish can be uneven in quality among the different species. Two species that are good for table fish are the amberjack of the southern Atlantic and the jack mackerel of the Pacific; the latter fish is often canned.

JEWFISH See Grouper.

KINGFISH See Mackerel.

LINGCOD See Greenling.

LOBSTER There are two species available in this country: The Northern or American or "Maine" lobster, found mainly off New England; and the spiny, or rock lobster, which is found on the Atlantic and Gulf coasts, with a very similar species found on the Pacific Coast. The spiny lobster, unlike the Northern, has no claws and most of its meat is in its tail. In this country, frozen spiny lobster tails are marketed as South African rock lobster tails. Both species range in size from 1 to 5 pounds.

MACKEREL The mackerel is a fatty saltwater fish, with a strong flavor and some dark flesh. Some of the most important species for food are: the Atlantic mackerel, found off the North Atlantic Coast and at its prime in the fall; the king mackerel, also called kingfish, which is seasonal in North Carolina and Florida; and the Spanish mackerel, best in winter and spring in Florida and Gulf waters.

MAHI-MAHI See Dolphin.

MONKFISH This ugly, bizarre-looking fish is also known as angler, devil, or frog fish. It is caught from Newfoundland to South Carolina and can weigh up to 50 pounds, but only the tail section is utilized. Monkfish is often called the poor man's lobster due to its firm texture.

MOONFISH See Cusk.

MULLET A saltwater fish with a mild white flesh that is moderately fatty. Species of mullet are found on both coasts; the striped mullet of the Atlantic and the silver mullet of the Pacific are the most important commercially. See also Sucker.

MUSKELLUNGE See Pike.

MUSSELS A bivalve mollusk found in both salt and fresh water, though only saltwater mussels are edible. The most common species is the blue mussel, found in seaside beds on both coasts (the "beards" of garnered mussels are the remnants of threads that anchor them to their beds). The mussel is rich in protein, vitamins, and minerals and can be substituted for clams in many recipes. Mussels are best in late fall, winter, and early spring, before spawning. They can be toxic as a result of pollution or certain feeding conditions—if you plan to gather them, check to be sure they are not under quarantine by your state fishing authority.

OCEAN PERCH An Atlantic Ocean rockfish that is important as a market fish. The Pacific rockfish is also called Pacific Ocean perch; see Rockfish.

OCTOPUS A mollusk that is neglected in the United States but is considered a delicacy in other countries. The meat of the octopus is mild in flavor and has been compared to chicken in taste. There are both Pacific and Atlantic species.

ONO See Wahoo.

OPAKA-PAKA This fish is a great delicacy of the Hawaiian people, who call it Hawaiian pink snapper. Found in the rocky coral of the Fiji, Samoa, and Hawaiian islands, it is good grilled or baked.

ORANGE ROUGHY This fish, found in New Zealand and Tasmania at depths of 2,000 to 4,000 feet, usually weighs around 3½ pounds. It is caught from May to July and October to February and is available in the United States only as a frozen fillet. The flesh is firm and white with a mild bland taste. It can be prepared like flounder and sole.

OYSTERS An oyster is a bivalve, cradled in a craggy shell, that does nothing all day but pump water, 50 to 100 pounds of water daily, depending on its size. As a consequence, an oyster tastes like the water and algae that has passed through it. Oysters divide into four major species: the Pacific or Japanese (*Crassostrea gigas*) with such names as Kumamoto, Willapa, Hog Island, Golden Mantle, and Westcott; the eastern (*Crassostrea virginica*) including Blue Points, Caraquets, Malapeques, Apalachicolas, and Gulf; Belon (*Ostrea edulis*), a European oyster grown on both the East and West coasts; and Olympia (*Ostrea lurida*), the indigenous West Coast species.

Natural oyster beds form along tidal shorelines where salty ocean water mixes with fresh river water. Because most oysters now are seeded and cultivated, there is very little risk of pollution. Most are started in warehouses, then transferred to bays.

Sometimes before they are fully grown they are moved from one bed to another where the minerals are richer, to fatten them up and give them their final flavor.

Oyster farming is undergoing a resurgence particularly on the West Coast, where most oysters are grown by cultivation. Less aquaculture is being done on the East Coast, where a lot of the oyster beds are natural fisheries, which are being affected by pollution and overfishing.

PERCH Several fish given the name perch, such as white perch and ocean perch, are not really members of this family. Two of the most important members of the perch family are the walleye and the yellow perch—both are fresh-water fish and are especially fine food fish, being caught both commercially and by sportsmen. The walleye is a migratory fish, sometimes called "yellow pike"; it is distinguished by its milky eyes and is found in the northeast quarter of the United States and in Canada. The walleye has a mild-flavored white flesh and can be substituted in any recipe calling for sole. The yellow perch has a firm white flesh and is found in the northern and central Atlantic states and in the Great Lakes area; it usually ranges from 1/2 to 2 pounds in size.

PETRALE See Sole under Flounder.

PICKEREL See Pike.

PIKE A fine table fish, with lean, firm white flesh, the pike is prized in Europe and is the traditional fish for *quenelles*. The two main varieties in the United States are the northern pickerel, usually 4 to 10 pounds in weight, and the muskellunge, usually 10 to 30 pounds. The pike is a freshwater sport fish, especially in the spring in the Northeast and upper Midwest; it is shipped commercially from Canada and is available fresh year-round.

PLAICE See American Plaice under Flounder.

POLLOCK See Cod.

POMPANO A silvery Atlantic Coast fish, the pompano is a favorite sport fish in Florida from October to May, ranging in size from 1-1/2 to 5 pounds. The pompano is prized as a table fish; it is generally rich in flavor, with a firm flesh and a moderate fat content.

PORGY A saltwater fish, important commercially and also fished for sport. Most porgies are lean, with a mild-flavored, tender flesh. Atlantic Coast porgies include the jolthead porgy, the red porgy, the sheepshead, and the whitebone porgy. The most common porgy on the Atlantic Coast is the scup, a silvery fish averaging 1 pound in size and most abundant in the summer months. There is one porgy on the West Coast, the Pacific porgy, but it is not common and not comparable to eastern porgies in table quality.

PORKFISH See Grunt.

PRAWN Jumbo shrimp are often misnamed prawns. The United States has a large fresh-water prawn, native to the South, but it is not available commercially.

PUMPKINSEED See Sunfish.

REDFISH See Red Drum under Drum.

RED SNAPPER See Snapper.

ROCK BASS See Sunfish.

ROCK COD See Rockfish.

ROCKFISH A Pacific Coast saltwater fish often sold as red snapper or rock cod. True rockfish include the Pacific ocean perch and the bocaccio. The rockfish is low in fat content and has a mild-flavored, firm flesh; it ranges from 2 to 5 pounds in size. Red snapper, ocean perch, and sea bass may be substituted for rockfish. See also Striped Bass.

SABLEFISH A fatty fish of the North Pacific, incorrectly called "black cod." The sablefish has a mild-flavored, very soft flesh and averages 30 to 35 pounds in weight.

SALMON The salmon is one of the most prized of all table fish, with a flavorful, fatty flesh that is rich in vitamin A and the B vitamins. Salmon are saltwater fish that ascend freshwater rivers and streams to spawn; there are also landlocked fresh-water salmon. The Atlantic salmon is no longer found in abundance in the Atlantic states because of pollution; most East Coast market salmon is shipped from Canada. Salmon is still abundant in the Northwest. The best salmon is caught in the ocean or very early in its migration upriver. There are five Pacific salmon: The chinook or king salmon is the largest of the species and is considered the premium salmon; its color varies in depth. The coho or silver salmon is considerably smaller than the chinook and its flesh is usually pink. The sockeye has a deep color and is sometimes called "blueback" salmon. The chum salmon and the pink salmon are the least expensive of the salmons. Recently, Norway has become a major source for salmon marketed in North America.

SANDDAB See Pacific Sanddab under Flounder.

SARDINE The sardine may be any one of several small species of the herring family. The Pacific sardine is now so scarce that it is no longer commercially fished; Atlantic sardines are commercially fished off the Maine coast and are occasionally available

fresh in eastern markets although most are canned.

SCALLOP A bivalve saltwater mollusk prized for its adductor muscle. There are several species of scallops with varying shell colors. The sea scallop of the North Atlantic Coast is the most commercially important; the bay scallop is 3 to 4 times smaller and is found in shallow waters from North Carolina to the Gulf of Mexico. There are several species of scallops on the Pacific Coast, including the rock scallop, but none are commercially important.

SCROD See Cusk.

SCUP See Porgy.

SEA BASS True sea bass include the black sea bass, sometimes called "blackfish," and the southern, bank, and rock sea basses. These are Atlantic Coast saltwater fish, usually marketed at 1-1/2 to 3 pounds. The sea bass has firm white meat with a mild flavor and is suitable for cooking by almost any method. Chilean sea bass is now widely distributed in North America.

SHAD A member of the herring family, the American shad is a saltwater fish that ascends rivers in winter and spring to spawn. It ranges from 1-1/2 to 7 pounds in size and is available fresh in southern markets December through March and in northern markets March through May. Though it has been introduced on the Pacific Coast it is utilized there mainly as a sport fish. The shad is prized for its roe; its flesh is flavorful, firm, and high in fat content. Two rows of extra "floating" (not part of the backbone) bones on each side of the shad must be cut out in strips after the fish is filleted.

SHARK A common food fish in many cultures, the shark is just beginning to be marketed in this country. The meat is firm and similar to the meat of the swordfish. The most valued of the sharks are the mako shark and the blue shark.

SHEEPSHEAD See Freshwater Drum under Drum; see Porgy.

SHIBI See Ahi under Tuna.

SHRIMP Shrimp are found on both coasts of the United States; the most important fishing areas are the South Atlantic and the Gulf of Mexico, and Alaska. Species include the miniature bay or ocean shrimp, most commonly sold already cooked and shelled at a count of 150 to 180 per pound. There are approximately 45 to 65 small shrimp per pound and 30 medium shrimp to a pound; jumbo or large shrimp, often called prawns, may number 6 to 16 per pound. Two pounds of raw shrimp in the shell will yield about 1 pound cooked and shelled shrimp.

SMELT A silvery saltwater fish, usually 6 to 8 inches long. The most common species is the rainbow smelt, found on both coasts. The smelt migrates upriver to spawn; it is also found landlocked in fresh water. Smelt is fished both commercially and as a sport fish during its spring spawning runs. Pacific Coast species are the eulachon or candlefish, and the surf fish. The bones of the smelt are soft enough that the fish can be eaten whole.

SNAPPER Snappers are found in the South Atlantic and the Gulf of Mexico. The red snapper is usually marketed at 4 to 6 pounds. This fish has a red skin and red eyes and a lean white flesh; it can be cooked by almost any method. Other snappers include the mutton, the vermilion, the gray, the schoolmaster and the yellowtail snappers.

SOLE A saltwater flat fish, the true sole is the Dover, or English, sole, usually available only frozen in this country. See Flounder.

SPECKLED PERCH See Sunfish.

SPOTTED SEATROUT See Weakfish under Drum.

SQUID A high-protein mollusk with 10 tentacles, this shellfish is found on both coasts. It is considered a delicacy in Mediterranean and Oriental cuisines.

STRIPED BASS A saltwater fish of both coasts, available fresh August through October. The striped bass ascends rivers to spawn and is also found landlocked in fresh water. It is most commonly found in Oregon and northern California and on the Mid-Atlantic Coast. A very popular sport fish in the East, it is often called "rockfish" there. The striped bass has a mild-flavored flesh that is low in fat; it ranges in size from 2 to 50 pounds but is best at a weight of 6 to 8 pounds. Two small fresh-water basses are related to the striped bass: the white bass and the yellow bass.

STURGEON The fish from which the roe for making caviar is taken. The sturgeon is found on both coasts in both fresh and salt waters; it has a firm flesh and can be substituted in recipes calling for swordfish.

SUCKER A lean fish with firm white meat, the sucker is found across the United States in fresh water. Its name derives from its manner of feeding by sucking food up into its large mouth. The sucker is usually sold at 3 to 5 pounds. Small suckers are sometimes sold as "mullet"; buffalos or buffalo-fish are larger suckers that can be substituted for carp.

SUNFISH The sunfish is a very popular fresh-water sport fish that is widely distributed throughout the United States and is often known as "bream." The most popular sunfish is the bluegill, which averages 6 ounces to 1 pound. The crappie, sometimes called a speckled perch, is a favorite in the

Midwest and South and averages 1 to 2 pounds. Other sunfish include the pumpkinseed, the redbreast and redear sunfishes, and the rock bass or goggle-eye. These small fish are good cooked whole or butterfly-filleted.

SURF FISH See Smelt.

SWORDFISH A saltwater fish found on both coasts and available fresh in summer and fall. The meat of the swordfish is firm and fully-flavored and is excellent broiled or baked.

TROUT A fresh-water fish, with sea-running forms of certain species. Trout are commercially farmed and are popular throughout the United States as a sport fish. Some "trout," such as the brook, lake, blueback, and Dolly Varden trouts, are really chars, fish so closely related to the trout family that they may be considered true trout.

Brook Trout Thought to be the best table trout, these average 1 pound or less. The sea-running brook trout is called a sea trout.

Brown Trout This fish averages 1 to 2 pounds; the sea-running brown trout is also known as a sea trout.

Cutthroat Trout Found in the North-west and the northern Rockies, the cutthroat averages 1 to 1-1/2 pounds. Its name derives from the red markings on its lower jaw.

Dolly Varden Trout A colorful speck-led trout found in the Northwest and the mountain states. This trout is named after a Dickens character who wore a pink-spotted dress. Average weight: 2 to 3 pounds.

Golden Trout Found in mountain streams at high altitudes in the West. The flesh of this trout ranges in color from coral to scarlet.

Lake Trout This trout has a fatty flesh and averages 10 to 20 pounds. It is found in the northern United States, Canada, and Alaska.

Rainbow Trout The most important trout commercially, the rainbow is native to the western United States. It averages 1 to 2 pounds in size. The sea-running form of the rainbow is the steelhead, which averages 6 to 12 pounds and has a pink flesh.

TOTUAVA See Weakfish under Drum.

TUNA A migratory saltwater fish that grows to huge sizes in some species, the tuna was an important food fish in the ancient world. It is more common-ly sold fresh in other countries than in the United States, where it is usually canned. Tuna is high in protein, with a flavorful, meat-like flesh. It can be poached, baked, or broiled, and is ex-cellent for *sashimi*. The two most im-portant commercial species are:

Ahi This fish is actually a yellow-tailed tuna, known in Japan as shibi. It is the most gaily colored tuna, with a long bright yellow dorsal and anal fins, and a stripe of golden yellow on its side. Ahi is found in tropical and subtropi-cal waters throughout the world. It is known as Rabil in Spain, Atun Ama-rillo in Mexico, and Tonnas Macryp-terus in Greece.

Albacore The albacore has the lightest flesh of all the tunas. It is found in both the Atlantic and Pacific, ranging from temperate to tropical waters. The Pacific albacore migrates between the Pacific Coast and Japan and is found fresh in western markets in late sum-mer and early fall.

Yellowfin Tuna This tuna is found on both coasts, generally in tropical and subtropical waters. It is the basis of the tuna industry in California.

Other species include the blackfin tuna, a good food fish found in the Atlantic; the bluefin tuna, which is the largest tuna; and the bonita, which has a dark flesh and is not marketed as a tuna.

TURBOT See Flounder.

TUSK See Cusk.

WAHOO This fish is the same as ono, which means "sweet" in Hawaiian. It is also known as the gourmet's mack-erel. The fish resembles the king mackerel in its long slender shape and, when cut, can be distinguished by a prominent vertical bar on its side. The flesh is white, of fine circular flake, and delicately textured.

WALLEYE See Perch.

WEAKFISH See Drum.

WHITE SEABASS See Weakfish under Drum.

WHITEBAIT Tiny immature saltwater fish of different species that may include herrings and anchovies. They are eaten whole.

WHITE BASS See Striped Bass.

WHITEFISH A fresh-water fish with a mild-flavored white flesh. The whitefish is a member of the salmon and trout family; species include:
Cisco A small whitefish found in lakes and fished both commercially and for sport. The cisco is marketed in the United States as "chub" and is usually sold in smoked form.
Lake Whitefish The most important whitefish commercially, it averages 3 pounds and is found in the Northeast and the North central states.

WHITE PERCH See Freshwater Drum under Drum.

WHITE SEABASS See Drum.

WHITING A market name for some species of hakes, usually silver hakes; see Hake under Cod.

YELLOW BASS See Striped Bass.

YELLOW PERCH See Perch.

YELLOW PIKE See Perch.

FAT CONTENT OF FISH

The fat content of fish is the result of several variables, and may differ among fish belonging to the same species. Factors affecting fat content include the age of the fish, the time of year the fish is caught, and the geographical area in which the fish is located. The following list is a general guide that includes both generic and specific names and is based on these categories: lean fish (an average fat content of 2 percent, based on a range of .1 to 3.9); moderately fatty fish (an average fat content of 6 percent, based on a range of 4 to 8.9 percent); and fatty fish (an average fat content of 12 percent, based on a range of 9 percent and above).

LEAN FISH

Black Bass	Hake
Brook Trout	Halibut
Bullhead	Jewfish
Burbot	Lingcod
Catfish	Muskellunge
Cisco	Ocean Perch
Cod	Pacific Sanddab
Crappie	Pike
Croaker	Plaice
Dolphin	Pollock
Drum	Porgy
Flounder	Rockfish
Grouper	Sea Bass
Haddock	Smelt
Snapper	Walleye
Sole	Whitefish
Spotted Seatrout	White Seabass
Striped Bass	Whiting
Sucker	Yellowfin Tuna
Sunfish	Yellow Perch
Turbot	

MODERATELY FATTY FISH

Albacore	Pigfish
Alewife	Pink Salmon
Bluefin Tuna	Pompano
Bonita	Rainbow Trout
Carp	Sablefish
Chum Salmon	Sea Trout
Dolly Varden Trout	Sturgeon
Eulachon	Swordfish
Freshwater Drum	Weakfish
Mullet	

FATTY FISH

Bluefish	Lake Trout
Butterfish	Mackerel
Chinook Salmon	Sablefish
Coho Salmon	Sardine
Eel	Shad
Herring	Sockeye Salmon
Jack Mackerel	Steelhead

NUTRITIONAL CONTENT OF FISH

A Comparison of the Nutritional Composition
of Meat, Fish, and Shellfish
Based on 1-Ounce (28 gram) Portions

g = grams
mg = milligrams
IU = International Units

	Calories	Protein g	Carbohydrate g	Fat g	Saturated fatty acids g	Polyunsaturated fatty acids g	Cholesterol g	Calcium mg	Phosphorus mg	Iron mg	Sodium mg	Potassium mg	Vitamin A IU	Thiamin mg	Riboflavin mg	Niacin mg
MEAT																
Lean Meat (6% fat)	80	7	0	7	1.4	.2	25	3	50	.8	17	70	13	.02	.06	1.3
FISH																
Lean Fish (2% fat)	24	5.5	0	.3	.06	.1	19	3	51	.2	19	96	95	.01	.01	.5
Moderately Fatty Fish (6% fat)	32	5.5	0	1.1	.31	.44	19	5	70	.2	38	149	93	.01	.02	2.4
Fatty Fish (12% fat)	60	6.4	0	3.8	.65	1.3	24	22	117	.3	33	126	45	.05	.02	2.4
SHELLFISH																
Clams	27	3.1	1.7	.26	.05	.05	14	20	42	2.1	58	51	28	.03	.05	.37
Crab	27	4.9	.31	.7	.07	.16	28	13	52	.23	28	31	615	.05	.02	.79
Lobster	25	4.9	.08	.4	.04	.29	28	18	52	.2	60	51	0	.02	.02	0
Oysters	21	2.4	1.4	.6	.21	.23	3	27	35	1.6	21	34	88	.04	.05	.71
Shrimp	30	6.6	.19	.4	.07	.15	42	33	96	.85	75	135	0	.03	0	0

Compiled from *Nutritive Value of American Foods in Common Units*, Agriculture Handbook No. 456,
United States Department of Agriculture

Index

BIOGRAPHICAL NOTES

LOU SEIBERT PAPPAS is the food editor of the *Times Tribune* in Palo Alto, California. A former food consultant for *Sunset* magazine, she now writes for other national food magazines and is the author of many other cookbooks, including *The New Harvest* and *The New American Chefs*. She has traveled extensively throughout the world collecting recipes for her books.

MARINELL AND ROBERT HARRIMAN are a team of free-lance designers and illustrators. They are both graduates of Chouniard Art Institute in Los Angeles, where they met. Their work has appeared in numerous publications.